To: the Honourable, Dr. Sahadeo BASDEO,
Minister of External Affairs & International
trade.
With very ber~ ...

Yussuff Hamidd
Port of Spain
28 Oct. 1988.

Speeches by Errol Barrow

edited by Yussuff Haniff

 A Hansib Publication

"...We have learnt one lesson and one lesson alone, that is how not to live together in unity.
We have evolved a formula for living together, but not having any strength. This is one of the paradoxes of our colonial situation in Barbados...
The soul of this community has to be laid bare, and there is no better time to do that than when we are preparing for independence, so that we know what we are, who we are, and where we are going."

Errol Walton Barrow
January 4, 1966

© Yussuff Haniff, 1987

First published in 1987 by Hansib Publishing Limited

Cover Design: Michelle Wilson
Production: Hansib Publishing Limited, 139/149 Fonthill Road, London N4 3HF, Tel: 01 281 1191, Telex: 22294, Fax: 01 263 9656

Printed in England by: Hansib Printing Limited, Unit 19, Caxton Hill Industrial Estate, Hertford, Hertfordshire, Tel: 0992 553592

ISBN: 1 870518 70 5

*To the marvellous people of Barbados
– who else?*

Contents

List of illustrations

Page

Acknowledgements

The publication of this book would not have been possible without the co-operation and encouragement of many individuals and institutions. I wish to thank Mr Clarence ("Coloured") Ward for his assistance in providing an almost endless supply of tape recordings of speeches of the late Errol Walton Barrow. The Ministry of Foreign Affairs, particularly the information section, was extremely helpful in providing the text of some of the speeches delivered outside of Barbados. The staff of the reference department of the Barbados Public Library and the Barbados Archives Department were also very helpful, efficient and patient. Without their assistance this work would not have been as extensive as it is.

The Caribbean Development Bank was also helpful in providing speeches and some photographs. Nation Printers Limited and the library of the *Nation* newspapers provided prompt and efficient assistance for all but a few of the photographs, whilst credit for the colour photograph on the front cover goes to Carrington Photo Creations Limited.

I also wish to thank Dr Erskine Simmons MD, the DLP member of parliament for the St Michael south east constituency and a good friend of mine, who provided strong encouragement and support for this work as did Mr Carlton Braithwaite, a close personal friend of the late Prime Minister Barrow. Attorney, David Commissiong generously provided important legal advice and a great deal of encouragement and support as well.

I wish to thank Arif Ali for readily agreeing to publish this book and for sharing my own enthusiasm. Thanks also to his personal assistant, Miss Jenny Lawther, for her advice and suggestions along the way.

A final word of thanks must of course go to my wife Brenda and children Ayesha, Corey and Craig, for their patience during the year's work involved in producing this volume.

Errol Walton Barrow

Born: 21st January, 1920
Died: 1st June, 1987

Errol Walton Barrow dominated the political life of Barbados through much of three decades and, in that time, played a major role in fashioning the way Barbadians viewed themselves and the way they saw their brothers and sisters in the Caribbean.

His was the gospel of self-reliance, self-esteem, and independence. He always sought an opportunity to remind the people of the Caribbean of their own capacity to solve their problems:

"We have been a people who have been imbued with a sense of our own inadequacy", Errol Barrow complained when he addressed the 1973 Caribbean Community Treaty signing ceremony in Trinidad and Tobago. Many of his speeches were designed to disabuse peoples' minds of this sense of inadequacy and to build up the self-confidence, not only of Barbadians, but of the peoples of the Caribbean in general.

His parting words to his fellow leaders in the Caribbean Community, delivered in Georgetown, Guyana in July 1986, amounted to a virtual statement of the principles which guided him: the uncompromising stand on the side of Caribbean independence and sovereignty; the need for the region to move closer together and to involve the masses of the people all the way; the need to harness the creativity of the people of the area to solve the problems of the day, and the need to put renewed emphasis on self-reliance.

Errol Barrow's adult life was one of service. He spent seven years in the Royal Air Force starting in 1940, and consequently saw service in the Second World War.

He returned home equipped with a degree in law and joined the then ruling Barbados Labour Party, serving as one of its members in Parliament from 1951 to 1955.

However in 1955 he led a breakaway group from the BLP, and formed the Democratic Labour Party (DLP). Six years later the party swept to power and held office for 15 unbroken years.

In those 15 years, Errol Walton Barrow presided over a quiet revolution in Barbados that transformed the society and opened up education opportunities to the masses of poor, black Barbadians by offering them free education from primary level through to university.

The mass outpouring of grief that followed his death was testimony to the high esteem in which he was held. The debate about a suitable memorial for him has brought suggestions ranging from changing the island's name to Barrow-bdos to erecting a life-sized statue in place of that of Lord Nelson in Bridgetown.

But the real testimony to Errol Walton Barrow's contribution to Barbados are the thousands of poor black people – the "submerged tenth" in his words – who now find education within their reach and, through education, a better life for themselves and their children.

M. Yussuff Haniff

Errol Walton Barrow – Patriot, Friend of working people and outstanding politician

A tribute by Michael Manley

In a world increasingly dominated by the superpowers there is a tendency for it to be assumed by the unthinking that the personalities of political significance are to be found only amongst the ranks of the mighty. At the same time the interaction between the democratic political process, the power of the mass media and the influence of the opinion poll is producing a kind of politician whose mediocrity reflects the perpetual search for compromise and the need to be all things to all people.

The Caribbean continues to confound both these assumptions. Earlier in this century Jamaica's Marcus Garvey fired the imagination of the black world, laying the foundations for the independence movements in the African homeland and the struggle for rights and recognition throughout the diaspora.

Trinidad's George Padmore played a vital role, building upon psychological foundations which Garvey had laid, in the development of the various political institutions which waged and eventually won the struggle for independence in Africa.

In the Caribbean itself Alexander Bustamente, Uriah Butler, and many others threw down the gauntlet on behalf of the working classes, the most direct victims of colonial exploitation. Norman Manley, T. A. Marryshaw, Grantley Adams and others issued the demand for political independence and commenced to fashion the political organisations which would first win and later manage freedom.

Caribbean nationalism was, accordingly, born of the need to create societies founded in freedom. Similarly, Caribbean politics proceeded on the assumption that freedom must open the doors to social justice. Finally, there emerged early a consensus concerning democracy as the means by which the people would pursue both justice and self-realisation.

Nationhood would not be achieved without struggle, thus the 1940s were a time of ferment and trouble in Barbados and the wider Caribbean.

At the same time, there were a few people of vision who, while committed to the ideals of nationhood for their own territories, also saw that the aspirations of the workers for a better life and the people as a whole for a world with larger horizons could be better served by a region united than by one divided into a number of parts. Standing tall in this company was Errol Walton Barrow.

Errol Barrow yielded pride of place to no person in his support for workers' causes. The long friendship and close association between himself and Sir Frank Walcott of the Barbados Workers' Union and, in the eyes of many, the dean of Caribbean trades unionists, is ample evidence of the late Prime Minister's commitment. That Errol Barrow was a deep, passionate and unwavering Barbadian statesman is impatient of debate. He was as unapologetically Barbadian as any person one could ever hope to meet. However, the region has produced countless men and women who reflected this peculiarly Caribbean sense of social justice and national independence as two sides of a single coin. What set Errol Barrow apart was his understanding that social justice must rest upon economic foundations if it is to be more real than rhetorical. This led him, in turn, to a commitment to economic integration as the only viable framework within which economic development could be pursued. Following the same inexorable logic, Barrow grasped the relationship between a regional economic framework and a political environment in which the sovereignty so newly won by the Caribbean could be defended.

It can be seen, therefore, that the commitment to social justice led his pragmatic mind to the conclusion that economic development pursued in a regional context would best accommodate the demands which social justice makes upon the body politic. At the same time his patriotism led him to examine the nature of sovereignty and in particular how this could best serve regional economic development and, no less important, how that sovereignty might best be defended.

To those who knew him, therefore, it came as no surprise that whether in opposition or upon his resumption of power, Errol Barrow opposed the invasion of a piece of English-speaking Caribbean soil by forces of the United States of America. Of equal logic and force was his unrelenting insistence that the Caribbean should be a zone of peace and not an area for ever-increasing penetration by foreign forces, from whatever source and however cunningly disguised. I believe that history will vindicate him abundantly on both scores.

By the same token his avowed intention upon his return to power of working to rebuild CARICOM trade and the integration process were simple extensions of his philosophy and his view of the Caribbean and its possibilities.

It is in his unrepentant view of the invasion of Grenada, along with his unswerving commitment to regional co-operation and to peace, that we find the final evidence of the qualities which made Errol Barrow so special. For he was, in truth, more than a politician in the ordinary sense of one circumscribed by the narrowest interpretation of what is immediately possible. Like all great politicians, who we choose inaccurately to rename as statesmen, Barrow made all his calculations of short-term political advantage subject to his deeper principles and the causes which they led him to uphold.

He will be remembered as the man who led Barbados into independence. He will be extolled as the author of free education and many other elements of the welfare state re-enacted in this tiny island in the Caribbean. But his claim upon history will extend far beyond the boundaries of Barbados. He will take his place amongst the significant heroes of Caribbean history. When we are brought finally by circumstance, by common heritage and by the logic of history to the point where we are the region which was foreseen by the deeper thinkers of the '30s and '40s he will take his place as a major architect of the process.

So much for the politics of the man. To the countless people who regarded themselves as privileged to share Errol Barrow's friendship, he was a very special person. Typically Barbadian, he had a dry wit and seemingly inexhaustible reserve of good humour. A hearty raconteur, the exterior of humour and story telling were often a facade for a nature generous to a fault. Once you were his friend, it were as though loyalty were underwritten in perpetuity.

Then, again, there was his intellect. A man of wide reading and real scholarship, he could confound his opponents with a flash of repartee. He was equally quick to deflate the windbags of humbug, who litter any political scene, with a single thrust, no less cutting because of the laugh with which he could round off some sally of wit. When he died, we mourned a significant patriot and grieved for a true friend.

Michael Manley

Michael Manley, former Prime Minister of Jamaica, was a close personal friend of Errol Barrow and is the political leader of the People's National Party of Jamaica.

Insurance for the pedestrian

First address in Parliament, on 7 February, 1952, as the senior member for St. George. (Barrow was then a member of the Barbados Labour Party (BLP).)

Sir, I do not think that many members of the general public who have listened to this debate in this chamber today, and I doubt whether many members of this House, really appreciate all the ramifications of this bill. Some honourable member – I cannot remember who it was – made some reference to the Third Party Insurance Act being on all-fours with the with the Workmens' Compensation Act. Mr Speaker, nothing could be further from the truth. Whereas the spirit of that legislation, and its objects and motives might have been similar to this legislation, this Bill seeks to place the less fortunate members of the community, in so far as accidents being suffered, particularly by bread winners, may not cause suffering to their dependants; while the motives of the Workmens' Compensation Act may be similar, I disagree that the objects are in any way the same as this Bill.

I will first explain this point. This Bill indemnifies the user or driver or owner of any motor vehicle against any liability, and I use the word advisedly because it is a word which appears time and again in this Bill. Already many users and owners of motor vehicles in this island indemnify themselves by taking out insurance policies, but there is no enactment in the laws of this island which makes it compulsory for the driver of a motor vehicle to insure against Third Party risks, the third party being some person other than the insurance company on the first part and the driver or owner of the motor vehicle on the second part.

If I may give a simple illustration: If your Honour were proceeding along one of the more busy highways of this city and someone dashed across the road suddenly and Your Honour was not insured against Third Party risks, that unfortunate person would be entitled to go to the Courts of Law and sue Your Honour – I do not mean to be personal in any way – for negligence, for a breach of that care which has to be exercised by every user of the highways. If that person, his executor, administrator or dependents, recovered damages, he would then have to go against Your Honour's estate, if such exists, in order to indemnify himself, in order to execute the judgement of the Court. Your Honour can appreciate that if a man of straw such as myself, were driving a car along one of the more busy highways of this city, and were unfortunate enough to be involved in a collision with some even less fortunate person than myself being the third party, the injured person who recovered damages in the Court against me would not be any better off, because I have nothing to go against. The whole object of Third Party insurance is to make sure that there will be some fund for the injured party to go against.

I wonder if the dim light of revelation has dawned on the members of this Assembly yet. Before the unfortunate person who is injured can recover damages, he has to prove that the accident was due to negligence on the part of the person who was in charge of the car. That is why we must distinguish this Bill from the Workmens' Compensation Act; under that Act, if a workman is injured in the course of his employment as the result of an accident he is entitled to compensation whether the accident is due to his negligence or not. The employer has to indemnify the workman as long as the accident took place during the course of the workman's employment. There are over 7,000 reported cases of Workmens' Compensation in which the actual problems arising before the Courts were the problems of this nature: Was the injured person a workman under the Act? Did the accident occur during his employment? And did the accident occur out of his employment? But once these three essentials are proved, except in borderline cases as to the relation between master and servant and between the injured party and the employer, the workman was always entitled to compensation.

On the other hand, we are faced with the anomaly that in Barbados, if a man walks across the street in front of a motor car and he is injured and the other party sets up as his defence that the man's own negligence contributed to the accident, we have the rather inequitable doctrine which will deny that man the right to recover anything at all. You have to prove absolute negligence on the part of the person who knocked you down, but if he sets up that your negligence in any infinitesimal measure contributed to the accident, then you would not be entitled to recover anything at all. If the negligence of the car driver is 99 per cent, and the negligence of the pedestrian is only one per cent, the pedestrian recovers nothing at all.

We see, therefore, the anomaly to which I referred earlier in my speech; although we are passing an Act to make sure that an unfortunate person who is injured may have some fund to go against, he has to be successful in the Court of Law.

I do not think that insurance companies are run on the line of provident associations; my experience is that they always fight cases bitterly even when they have been advised by their own legal staff that they are in the wrong. As a matter of principle, they always resort to some legal subtlety in order to escape paying money out of their coffers. An insurance company does not like to settle claims outside the Court, and in nearly 100 per cent of the cases, the accidents will end by litigation: it is only when judgement is pronounced in the court that liability is brought home to the insurance company. I just want to say that it has been my experience in this island that we, with the best intentions have adopted certain social measures which have been enacted in the United Kingdom for the benefit of the different sections of the community and for the community as a whole, but very often we have adopted those measures without looking at the supporting and ancillary enactments which already exist in the United Kingdom so as to make these measures which we now propose a reality. I am suggesting, Mr Speaker, that instead of repeating the mistakes which we have made so many times in the past, we should, as soon as possible, enact a Law Reform Contributory Negligence Act which states, in my own words, that where any accident occurs which is partly due to the fault or default of the other party, instead of throwing the plaintiff or the injured party out of court because he has in some manner contributed to the cause of his injury, the Court would be entitled to allocate damages, as it were, in proportion to the extent to which each party has contributed to the injury. If one were riding a bicycle and by his negligence he contributed only 10 per cent towards the cause of the accident, and a motorist by his negligence contributed 90 per cent to the cause, instead of the cyclist being denied the right to recover any damages at all, he would recover nine-tenths of the damages which the court would normally have given him if he had not been contributory to his own injury.

That is the first point which I would like to make. There is another point which is not germane to the present issue; but, at some very early date, we shall have definitely to revise and amend the Separation and Maintenance Act, 1950 and make its provisions more widely known to the community. However, I do not intend to dwell on that issue, but having had a cursory glance at the present Act, I say that there are certain things which need to be amended.

To come back to the Bill before us, the various points will be gone into by a Select Committee. Far from Honourable Members on this side of the House being opposed to referring this Bill to a Select Committee, I would like to assure the Honourable Senior Member for the City that it was the intention of the members of the government to propose that the Bill may be referred to a Select Committee. The interest of the community must be considered and will always be considered by the members on this side of the House; if the members on the other side have made the proposals that this Bill will be referred to a Select Committee before we did so, we do not grudge them that bit of praise.

I was surprised that the honourable Member for the City even thought of referring this Bill to a Select Committee because we on this side have fully discussed this matter a long time ago. We have no intention to stampede or steam roller through this House legislation which is so far-reaching in its social consequences.

Although I am not going into the details of the Bill, in respect of Clause 4 (I) (b) (ii) some persons might be tempted to believe that it means that people who are riding on a bus and are injured would not be able to recover damages; but that is not so. That particular sub-clause refers to people who are merely joy-riding or who are friends or invitees of the driver of the vehicle. In Sub-Clause (n) (v) of the same Clause 4 – I would make this last point – the liability of the insurance company is limited to £1,000 sterling which is rather surprising; because if a person who is injured went to the Court and recovered £5,000 sterling damages, he would only be able to go against the insurance company to the extent of £1,000 sterling and would have to take proceedings against the injured himself for the other £4,000 sterling. There may be cases in which people may not be in a position to pay this amount, so that this particular sub-clause may seem to defeat the whole object of the Bill; but I understand that if the full liability of the insurance company were not limited, the premiums would be so high as to make it impossible for a normal member of the community like myself, who earns a moderate income, to subscribe to such a scheme.

But there is a penalty for not being insured; if the members of the community who own and drive cars are called upon to insure, then you have to make it possible for us to do so. I hope that since the recovery of damages under the Bill depends upon the success of litigants in the Courts of this island, the cost of litigation in the higher Courts of this island will soon be made less burdensome to the average citizen than it is at present.

"No taxation without representation"

Address in Parliament January 30, 1962, on the measure to lower the voting age from 21 to 18 years

It has been declared as part and parcel of the policy of members of this Party, and we had a mandate from the people, for the reduction of the voting age.

The honourable senior member for St Peter dealt exhaustively and courageously with this Bill not only on this occasion, but in 1961 when the Government rejected the one which he introduced and it is not necessary for me to go over the ground which he so adequately covered both in that debate and in this one.

When Her Majesty's Secretary of State for the Colonies was in Barbados not so long ago – within the last three weeks – we pointed out to him that we had got the mandate of the people for the reduction of the voting age and we were committed to supporting a Bill on the floor of the House by an honourable member for that purpose. The Secretary of State for the Colonies intimated to us that it was entirely a domestic matter, and in view of the fact that it would not be necessary to change anything in the Letters Patent or in the Instruments within which the Constitution of Barbados is written – such as the Executive Committee Act – it would be a matter for us to go ahead if we so cared.

When the matter was put before the Government, the then Solicitor General appeared to be of the opinion that the amendment would involve the preparation of three separate registers – a register for the Federal Government Elections, a register for Local Government Elections and a register for the General Assembly Elections. The law relating to the register for the Federal Government Elections – and I cannot see that it would be necessary in these present circumstances – is that the register for the Federal Government Elections, should be the Local Government Register as existing in January, 1958. Therefore, if the Federal Government Elections were to be held any time within the next six months, or I would say within the next twelve months, which in my opinion appears now to be extremely unlikely, the position would be that even although we made the amendment to the Representation of the Peoples Act in respect of this, it would not entitle those of the age of 18 years to 21 years to vote in the Federal Government Elections. However, I do not think that that election is one which should cause any concern because, as I have said before, it is extremely unlikely that such an election will take place. This, of course, is just a personal assessment of the situation according to the way things are shaping at the present moment.

When we come to the question of the Local Government Elections, we have just passed through the Local Government elections and we are not due to hold another election for Local Government Councils until the year 1964. That gives us adequate time to prepare a separate register or alternatively to amend the Local Government Act and perhaps any consequential amendments to other Acts. There again, I do not think that can be a valid objection to the passage of the Bill at this particular time.

However, it is obvious to anyone who has made a study of the Local Government Act that there are several provisions in that Act which are repugnant to our ideas of democratic government in Barbados – ideas of this Government and ideas which I am sure the honourable senior member for St Peter will be quite willing to support. There are several provisions in that Act which tend to make it appear that Local Government Elections are more important than the elections to the General Assembly of this Island. There is such a thing as the qualifications which they have laid down for one to be a member and there are other things such as the method of taxation, the relief which is granted to owners of plantations and matters of that kind. It is, therefore, obvious that several major amendments, in the light of the policy of the present Government would have to be made to the 1958 Local Government Act under which we are now suffering.

The procedure when a Private Bill is introduced is that that Bill should be sent to a Select Committee; this Bill, therefore, has to go to a Select Committee. When the Honourable Leader of the House made the motion, it was an act of supererogation on his part and, as one of my friends on my right would say, it was done out of an abundance of caution. It was, in the light of the provision of our standards, not entirely necessary, but it was only emphasising to honourable members that we do not intend to stampede Private Members' Business until both the public and the members of this House have had full opportunity to debate, discuss, analyse, criticise and make recommendations on measures of this kind. I have already given instructions that all the consequential amendments attendant upon the passage of the Bill, without in any way anticipating the will of the House, should be prepared, so that when the Select Committee reports, we will be able to introduce within a very short time, the legislative amendments which would make this provision for the reduction of the voting age to 18 years a practical proposition.

Mr Speaker, I entirely agree with the honourable senior member for St Peter that if there is any political illiteracy in this island, if there is any political agnosticism or atheism, it is to be found in the age-group 50 to 80 rather than in the 18 to 21 age-group. If there is any age group which has had the advantage of some kind of formal education to the extent of 100 per cent, that age-group must certainly be the one from 18 years to 21 years. I agree that in our archaic system of the Mosaic Law, a man can suffer capital punishment at the age of 18 years, he can marry at the age of 18 years, he is also subject to the payment of income tax, and if we follow the principle of no taxation without representation to its logical conclusion, it is clear that we cannot disenfranchise the people who are taxpayers of this colony. The average age of young people who are leaving school in Barbados is 14 years and in Secondary schools it is about 17-and-a-half to 18 years. We anticipate an economic condition in this country that young people will be absorbed in the avenue of gainful employment immediately on leaving the Secondary Schools and the Primary Schools of this island; if they are going to be absorbed in the avenues of employment, then they will become taxpayers and it is only logical that these young people should have some say in the running of the country in which they live. I, therefore, have great pleasure in supporting the second reading of the Bill which has been moved by the honourable senior member for St Peter, and it is only an indication that this Government does not intend to fall into the thinking of the previous government that whenever a private member introduces a Bill they would automatically oppose its passage. The past government has gone to the extent that they, rather than support legislative matters on the Order Paper, have prorogued the House so that they could kill every possible item of Private Members' Business on the Order Paper. We do not intend to follow that practice. We now see that members of the erstwhile Government are going into the reverse now; they no longer have the power to advise the officer administering the government of the country as to the dissolution of the Legislative Session; so they climb on the vanguard of the 'holier than thou-ers' or the new frontier men and they even second the motions moved by private members.

It is true that they are lagging rather far behind but we welcome them to our ranks in the same way that we would welcome the 18 to 20 years old into the ranks of the progressive way of the exercise of the franchise at the present time.

'You cannot draw up an indictment against a whole nation'

Statement to Parliament on June 19, 1962, introducing a resolution condemning the British government's suspension of the constitution of Grenada

An emergency meeting of the Cabinet of this island was held this morning because during the past twenty-four hours, there was released from London an Order-in-Council which indicated that the United Kingdom government had decided as from today's date, to suspend the constitution of the neighbouring territory of Grenada and to dissolve the Legislative and Executive Councils of that island.

I am sure that honourable members would forgive me and other members of the Cabinet if, as Westindians and if as persons who are looking forward to the eventual emancipation of the area from imperial rule under which we have suffered so long – and I make no apologies for stating unequivocally that I am anti-imperialist; as a matter of fact, even the leaders of the Conservative Party in the United Kingdom are anti-imperialists in their declaration when we see the rapidity with which they are dissolving the British Empire.

I, therefore, make no apology whatsoever to the members of the Opposition in this House, to the members of the public or to the United Kingdom government, if I reiterate what the general public already knows – that is, my stand in matters of this kind. I am not in favour of any form of imperialism, whether it is British imperialism, American economic imperialism, or Russian economic imperialism. I am opposed to imperialism in any form, shape or disguise, no matter from whatever quarter that imperialism happens to emanate. The terms of the resolution which the Cabinet has agreed upon, read as follows: –

'Resolved that this House strongly protests against the action taken under the authority of the Westindies Act, 1962, by the Government of

the United Kingdom in suspending the Constitution of Grenada and in dissloving the Legislative and Executive Councils of that island.'

Mr Deputy Speaker, that is the Resolution which we will be calling upon members of this House to support. I think, Sir, that you will forgive a little background history of the dissolution of the executive and legislative councils of Grenada and the drastic action which the United Kingdom has elected to pursue. Sometime in 1961, subsequent to the London Conference of that year, the United Kingdom, in its wisdom – and I use that word in its very loosest sense – decided to permit the re-enfranchisement of a gentleman, who, at one time, enjoyed the confidence of the majority of the electorate of the island of Grenada and who had been disenfranchised by the electoral law of that colony and was still suffering under the disability of that disenfranchisement.

Mr (Eric) Gairy, the Chief Minister of Grenada, attended the London Conference in 1961 as an adviser to the Government of Grenada, and it would appear to me that, with the connivance of the Colonial Office in London, the law under which Mr Gairy was suffering this disability was abrogated and a new enabling Act passed in the Grenada Legislature so that Mr Gairy – with whom the Colonial Office could have been in no agreement on any constitutional matter in view of the fact that it was the Colonial Office which had elected to banish Mr Gairy to the neighbouring island of Carriacou some seven or eight years previously – it was with this collaboration and connivance that the electoral law was flouted and the legislature was allowed to pass a Bill which enabled Mr Gairy to take over the reins of government in Grenada. That was taken by people in the outside world as an indication that the Colonial Office was, at that time, satisfied that Mr Gairy had manifested his intention to behave like a responsible politician and statesman and that the Colonial Office had now become enamoured of Mr Gairy's claim for leadership.

So said, so done, Mr Deputy Speaker; and after the victory of Mr Gairy's Party in the election campaign Mr Gairy was duly chosen as the Leader of his Party and as the elected leader of the people of Grenada. In that capacity, he attended all our conferences on federation and made some kind of contribution towards the conclusions at which we arrived at the London Conference held in May this year. Subsequent to the election of Mr Gairy as the leader of the Grenada Movement, the people of Jamaica manifested an intention to turn their backs on the rest – I should say, on the Eastern Caribbean – and to pull out, as it were, of the Federation which was then in existence by a Referendum held in the last quarter of last year, sometime around the 11th and the 13th of September. We all know from recent history that the United Kingdom government, after receiving a clear expression, not from the government of Trinidad or from the people of Trinidad – and I offer this as no criticism at all, although criticism may be justified; I am merely making a statement of fact as to what took place – after receiving, as I say, an expression from the General Council of the Peoples' National Movement which is the party of the government of Trinidad, a clear indication that, not one, but two members of the Federation of the Westindies were anxious to dissociate themselves from that most unfortunate grouping, it was at that stage that the United Kingdom government decided that the only thing which could be done in the circumstances was to break up the existing Federation in a manner which would leave no doubt as to its existence or non-existence.

Mr Deputy Speaker, I do not think that it would be entirely keeping faith either with history or with the members of the public in Barbados, if I did not disclose that there was no Westindian man or woman of goodwill who would be entirely in agreement with Mr Gairy; but it is clear that there is no Westindian politician in the Windward or Leeward Islands or Barbados with whom I happen to be associated at the time, who was in disagreement that steps should be taken to dissolve the existing Federation, provided that they were legitimate steps.

It was, moreover, the opinion of most people who had some kind of acquaintance with the constitutional aspects of the matter that as long as one member of the partnership withdrew from the partnership, the Association automatically ceased to exist. There was no provision in the Federal Constitution for a referendum, neither was there any provision for secession of any territory, neither was there any provision for a declaration to continue with the association of the territories at any stage; and in view of the fact that we have now considered that at this stage of the 20th century we could not, as some ill-advised persons and sections of the Press wanted people to do, that is, enforce the territory of Trinidad and the territory of Jamaica to remain in an association reluctantly, in view of all these considerations, Mr Deputy Speaker, I said – and I repeat – that not only were men and women of goodwill, but also responsible politicians with whom I happened to be associated, were in agreement with the dissolution of the existing Federation, and that is still our point of view.

The Federation as it then existed, moreover, had become associated and tainted with the suspicion that it was not working in the best interest of the Westindian people, particularly those people from the Windward and Leeward Islands and Barbados. So, Mr Deputy Speaker, amidst some kind of protest, but with firm resolve, the United Kingdom government pressed through first in the House of Lords and later in the House of Commons, a Bill which provided for the dissolution of the Federation, *inter alia*, a Bill which provided for the suspension of Unit constitutions, if necessary, and a Bill which was known at that time as the Westindies Bill, 1962, and later became the Westindies Act, 1962. Under Section five of this Act, an Order-in-Council was made in May, 1962 which dissolved the existing Federation.

We in Barbados as members of the government scrutinised the provisions of this Bill. Members of this Honourable House expressed fears that this Bill was capable of being employed as the thin edge of the wedge, which, driven right home, would divest Unit Legislatures of their constitutions and authoritative functions of presiding over their own destinies which they at that time happened to enjoy. It was because of these fears and because of our own suspicions that I decided on my own initiative, and after consultation with the members of my Cabinet, to address a telegram to the Secretary of State on the 21st of March, 1962, the contents of which I have already disclosed to the members of the House, but which perhaps, it would not be inopportune to read at this stage.

This telegram, Mr Deputy Speaker, reads as follows:

'While it may be necessary to make provision for certain limited aspects of government in individual islands consequent on dissolution of existing Federation, I strongly urge that to allay fears and dissipate suspicions you should give firm assurance – as result of my representations to you – that nothing will be done by Order-in-Council to render inferior or retrogressive the constitutional gains already achieved in Barbados, the Windward Islands or the Leeward Islands. As I am receiving almost daily protests from Chief Ministers of Leeward and Windward Islands, it would be greatly appreciated if assurance could be given immediately.'

No member of the House, therefore, could be in any doubt during the course of this debate as to what attitude I would adopt if an occasion such as the instant one arose. On the 26th March, some five days later, I received a Priority Telegram, also confidential, addressed to me which read as follows: –

'No. 60 PRIORITY Telegram No. 43
'WESTINDIES BILL
'PLEASE PASS FOLLOWING TO PREMIER.
'I can give you the assurance you are asking for in respect of Barbados. Indeed, the Minister of State speaking on Clause five in Lords on March 7th said: –

It is not the intention of H.M. Government to use any of the powers under this clause to derogate in any way from constitutional status those territories which are already enjoying full internal self-government.

'I cannot, however, give any such assurance in the case of the Windward and Leeward Islands. One of the effects of the Bill is to transfer responsibility for administration of grants-in-aid back to the United Kingdom. In the circumstance, I must have the power ultimately to ensure that moneys voted by Parliament are properly spent especially in view of growing evidence in recent months of mismanagement in some quarters. I shall be seeking for an opportunity in Parliament this week to make the point plain.'

You will notice, Mr Deputy Speaker, that that was a confidential telegram addressed to me personally; but as I have said on frequent occasions, except where the security of the realm is threatened, I do not believe in government by conspiracy; I believe in government by consent. I do not believe that the affairs of the people should be conducted in a conspiratorial atmosphere, and I consider that by addressing a confidential, private telegram to me, the Secretary of State was not aware of my attitude on matters of this kind, and if he was aware, he was placing me in a rather invidious pattern vis-à-vis, my other colleagues from the Windward and Leeward Islands. Because of this, I could not make a disclosure to the House as I had already some weeks ago indicated, and I sent another telegram to the Secretary of State which reads as follows: –

'FROM GOVERNOR ADDRESSED TO SECRETARY OF STATE
Sent 12th April, 1962 (1600)
No. 56 PRIORITY
'Your telegrams No. 60 Westindies Bill and No. 67 Conference of Eight.
'Following from Premier begins.
'Prior to receipt of your telegram I had promised the House of Assembly to make public your reply to my request for assurances regarding change of constitutional status of these islands by Order-in-Council. This promise received newspaper publicity and I must now say

what is your reply.

'Two. I am meeting Chief Ministers of Leewards and Windwards in Antigua April 16th to discuss arrangements for providing Migrant Services in U.K. on dissolution of Migrant Services division of the Westindies Commission in London and also to discuss the general situation in regard to Federation of the Eight. Chief Ministers are becoming increasingly restive at the present uncertainties.

'Three. Grateful if you would send me by telegram repeated to Administrator Antigua, a reply to be made public in Barbados as well as at the meeting of the Eight on April 16th.'

I received the next day from the Secretary of State for the Colonies the immediate telegram worded as follows: –

'Secretary of State
'Sent 13th April, 1962 (1640) Addressed to GOVERNOR.
'Received 13th April, 1962 (1500)
'No. 75 IMMEDIATE
'2. On the question of the exercise of powers under the Westindies Act, 1962, I have no objection to your releasing reply given in my telegram 60. You can also draw attention to my comments on this matter in Hansard on March 26th column 855 to 856 and April 2nd Columns 146 and 147.'

Mr Deputy Speaker, as soon as I received this reply from the Secretary of State for the Colonies, I came into this House and I disclosed the full background and all the relevant information. I also managed to secure in a remarkably short time, copies of Hansard for the relevant dates and I stated what the Secretary of State said in the House of Commons which was substantially in accordance with what he disclosed to me in his telegram, No. 60.

If I may be permitted just to sum up the attitude of the United Kingdom Government, it was that Clause Five of the Westindian Act of 1962, which was then a Bill – it had not yet become law – and which had been initiated by debate in the House of Lords and then filtered down to the lower regions of the House of Commons, gave the United Kingdom government power by Order-in-Council to dissolve the constitution of any Unit Legislature in the Westindies and to set up in substitution therefore some alternative form of government which would be entirely at the discretion of the United Kingdom government for as long a period as the United Kingdom in its discretion thought fit. It was also stated that these provisions were not meant to apply to the people of the island of Barbados, but they could give no assurance that they did not intend to use them against the Windward and Leeward Islands.

The effect of the disclosure which I was permitted to make was to make the people of the Windward and Leeward Islands view Barbados with a certain amount of suspicion, and the Barbados delegates at subsequent meetings of the Chief Ministers and their delegates, whether in the Westindies or in London, had the greatest difficulty in impressing upon the people of the Windward and the Leewards and their representatives that the Barbadians were not, if I may be colloquial, sucking up to the Colonial Office, that the age of Uncle Tom in Barbados was over and that we were no imperialistic stooges who were prepared to sell the other islands so that we could get some advantage for ourselves.

I think honourable members will bear me out that in reply to the Secretary of State for the Colonies at the London Conference, I had to remind him that it was not a question of not giving Barbados some special privilege, but that we were anxious to see that the constitutions of the other islands were brought up to the same constitutional advancement which we are now enjoying. We were accused by the same Mr Gairy of sitting down and not saying anything because we had been promised something, and I asked Mr Gairy what it was that the Secretary of State had to promise us which we did not have already. I asked that because in this colony we have only been inhibited for the past sixty years, not even for six months or fifteen years, by our own philosophy of accepting that certain things are not for us.

Even now, we have people in Barbados who do not understand the politics of nationhood and who are pusillanimous of the advantages of independence. Perhaps the only Barbadian politician who in the last sixty years can claim that he has done something for the constitutional advancement of this colony is the late Deputy Speaker, Mr A.E.S. Lewis, a former junior member for Bridgetown. He insisted at all times that Barbados had got to the stage where we should be given universal suffrage as the major and perhaps the only real constitutional advancement in Barbados in the twentieth century. The introduction of ministerial status, the paying of salaries to Ministers and to members of the house and such things, I do not regard as any substantial constitutional advancement because you should not have to ask anybody for those things. The Executive Committee Act of 1891, which I think is Chapter 22, is the real mainspring of the constitutional advancement of this island, although

I would like to disclose that I have not been an admirer of Sir Conrad Reeves who has been the author of that Act. However, we must recognise that this is the real instrument which puts control of the economy of this island firmly into the hands of the elected representatives of the people of this island.

Mr Deputy Speaker, I very much appreciate that you have permitted me to digress somewhat from the original theme, but I was merely pointing out that the telegram of the Secretary of State sent to me as Premier of Barbados, was one which I did not view with any joy at all, and I regarded it as another attempt, even although it may not have been done deliberately, to create the impression that there were two grades of citizens in the Eastern Caribbean: one, the citizens of Barbados, and the other, the citizens of the Windward and Leeward Islands. As I have said, with the assistance of the independent members of this Honourable House, like the honourable senior member for St Peter, the honourable junior member for St George, who attended one of our conferences, and the honourable leader of the Opposition, I think we were able in some measure to dispel some of the fears which existed in the minds of the leaders of the Windward and Leeward Islands.

During the currency of our discussions, both here and in London, a Commission of Enquiry had been set up to enquire into certain allegations of mismanagement by the government of Grenada in general, and by the Chief Minister in particular, at the instance of the Federal Government and a Barbadian judge was appointed to preside over that enquiry. That enquiry made one or two false starts, but if eventually got off the ground; and while we were in the middle of the conference in London, Mr Gairy, the Chief Minister of Grenada, was greatly agitated throughout the proceedings, and he could hardly sit in his place because the Sword of Damocles was hanging over his head: and if at times he appeared to be slightly on edge, we were very appreciative of the position in which he found himself and to which he could have somewhat contributed himself.

I am not making any pronouncement or passsing any judgement. When the report was released, it more or less castigated the Ministers and the Chief Minister of Grenada for mismanagement of public funds and for attempting to intimidate members of the public service of that island. The Commission made no recommendations whatsoever, neither was the evidence of the Commission published. Anyone who has any knowledge of the procedure of these Commissions of Enquiry or who has had a nodding acquaintance with the procedure in a Court of Law, anyone who has been aware of the publication of the reports of the Commissions of Enquiry in the island of Barbados would realise right away that that slender document, which was elevated to the plane of a Stationery Office Publication, issued by authority of the United Kingdom government – any such person would realise that that publication must have been a very much abridged version of the Report which must have been originally submitted to the United Kingdom government by the Commission of Enquiry.

It was a remarkable document in that none of the evidence was published, and it made no real recommendation except that there should be a tightening up of the financial provisions relating to the government of Grenada. When I was approached by members of the delegations, by members of the United Kingdom delegation as well as by other people in the United Kingdom as to what was going to happen when the Grenada Report was published, my answer was always the same. A Commission of Enquiry has no right (of) indicting anyone; the purpose of such a Commission is to bring in a forcible manner to public opinion any irregularities which may have been existing in the body politic. The next step was that, having elected not to proceed by way of indictment in a Court of Law, you set up a Commission of Enquiry because you do not consider that the behaviour complained of merits such a drastic step as the prosecution of an individual or of two or three or four persons, but it is a matter which is sufficiently grave that the electors of the area should be acquainted with and get their information on an authoritative level. That is my personal view of the invoking of the machinery of a Commission of Enquiry. I think it would be very high-handed for any government to short-circuit a legitimate prosecution of a person before the Courts of Law of the territory and save that person from incarceration or a fine or some kind of punishment which the law would demand, by setting up a Commission of Enquiry.

A Commission of Enquiry cannot act as a preliminary magistrate's investigation; you cannot set up a Commission of Enquiry and ask an Attorney General of an island to take proceedings on the findings, when the Commission has already fully ventilated a case in the public arena of the territory itself and right through the stratosphere; the matter is disseminated by the press and the radio, not only in the territory, but outside the territory as well.

Therefore, it would be placing a prosecutor in a highly invidious position if after a Commission of Enquiry has gone into the matter, he is asked to prosecute the case; the minds of the jury would have been prejudiced already. I do not know of any instance – there may be some – where a Commission of Enquiry in the island of Barbados has been followed by an indictment in the Courts of Law; that is why I say that one would only take the step of setting up a Commission of Enquiry if the matters complained of were of so nebulous a character or one did not consider them serious enough to make a public prosecution. One may allow public sentiment at election time to take control and decide who is wrong or who is right, or on the other hand, whether the people elect a particular person to manage their affairs, whether he mismanages them or not. The sovereignty of the electorate is such that the electorate sits down in Barbados and chooses people, even although it is manifest that those people are not acting in the interest of the masses who have put them there. We in Barbados have to suffer because of this built-in foundation in the democratic system of government – the freedom of the people, whose representatives may pass a law to expropriate property or send people to a cross. Each and everyone of us has paid that price by having governments who were not interested in carrying out the wishes of the people.

The purpose of my illustrations and argument is to demonstrate that having elected to set up a Commission of Enquiry as to what was going on in Grenada, it is clear that the Commission of Enquiry has not got the power to indict anyone. It would be highly undesirable for a prosecution to take place when the intention is to bring matters to public notice. My idea is that the gentlemen who were appointed to sit on the Commission of Enquiry were members of integrity, who had sifted the evidence, and they were making it available so that public sentiment and public opinion would be brought to bear on any future occasion that these mismanagers may offer themselves to the people. I have spent sometime explaining the background because I want my premises to be clear.

Unless members of this House understand the premises from which I am arguing they would not be able to understand the Resolution which is now before the House, and at this stage perhaps it would be advisable for me to state that this Resolution is in no way intended to condone or connive any mismanagement which may have taken place in the island of Grenada. But all of us feel as government ministers, having met in Cabinet and considered this matter from the constitutional and every other point of view from which it should be considered, that this is a matter for the people of Grenada themselves. It is not a matter for the Colonial Office or the people of Barbados whether they approve or disapprove. The ballot box is the place where this should be decided, and nothing should be done by anyone to try to influence the exercise by the voters of that territory of their democratic right to elect whatever form of government, whether it be a communist government, a fascist government, a democratic government or any other form of government that they want.

Mr Deputy Speaker, it is neither the business of the United Kingdom, the people of Barbados, the people of America, nor the people of the Soviet Union. It is a matter for the exercise by the people of Grenada of their democratic rights and privileges, and I want to get that clear, because if one does not understand that, this resoultion does not in any way cast aspersion on the integrity of the members of the Commission. I am prepared to accept that everything that the Commission said has been proven by the standard which is demanded in a Court of Law for all criminal offences. It has been proven without any reasonable doubt, because I do not imagine any of those gentlemen, knowing some of them in the way I know them, would accept any kind of third or fourth hand evidence that certain irregularities occurred in the matter of the finances in the colony of Grenada.

I am not a personal friend of the Chief Minister of Grenada, neither is he or anyone else my enemy. I am not prepared to defend the suppressing of the constitution, whether or not I agree with what he has done. I see only constitutional issues which are involved; and if any member of this Chamber wants to wash his hands of this matter and say that he could never agree with Gairy, and that he could never agree with what was done in Grenada, I am urging upon him that that is not what we are being called upon to consider now. What we are being called upon to consider is this: when you hear the bell ringing, ask not for whom the bell tolls: it only tolls for thee.

Mr Deputy Speaker, it is not my intention to continue any longer on this matter, because I am sure that other members both on this side and on the other side of this Honourable Chamber will want to express an opinion for or against this Resolution, and it is our intention to allow them to do so. I am sure that your honour will not in any way curtail debate on this matter, except in so far as your honour considers that a speaker is being irrelevant, or alternatively, that he is in breach of the Standing Orders of this House.

In order to highlight the action which we are asking the House to take, I want to invite honourable members to cast their minds back to certain similar actions on the part of the United Kingdom government. Now as you will know, the historian of my party is the Honourable Minister of Education (J. Cameron Tudor, now Foreign

Minister, Sir James Tudor). I am entirely innocent of any knowledge of historical dates, because from the time I was at school, I found it impossible to consider dates of any importance except roughly to indicate different phases in the world's history which may have taken place. But if I remember rightly, sometime between 1953 and 1954 the constitution of British Guiana was taken away by a Conservative government in the United Kingdom. I am reminded by the Honourable Minister of Education who is a walking encyclopaedia on these matters, that it was in October, 1953. If that date is wrong, he must take the responsibility for it; but according to him, in October 1953, the British government decided to take away the constitution of British Guiana after the British Guiana government had been in office for a mere six months.

Mr Deputy Speaker, the difference between that occasion and this one – or the differences, because there are several differences – are that on that occasion they were not alleging that there was any financial irregularity. I understand that a senior Government official who was an Englishman was invited to bring a glass of water for the now President of the Senate, and that they felt that was lowering the prestige of the public servants from the metropolitan country; not that that was the only reason, if that is a reason at all. But there were a lot of silly little bagatelles – somebody painting the statue of Queen Victoria in one of the streets of Georgetown, or somebody writing something on a wall. Well, Barbadians and people from England as well, are in the habit of writing all kinds of things inside the doors of public lavatories all the time, and no constitution is taken away for that. There were a lot of silly, annoying incidents which one would normally expect from a country like British Guiana – I am not being derogatory in any way – which did not have the long history of constitutional development which we have enjoyed in the island of Barbados. Here was a trading post of a company like the Hudson Bay Trading Company where the contractors carried their furs; British Guiana was the tropical trading post of the Hudson Bay Trading Company which suddenly found itself with a large measure of internal self-government after a fairly bitter struggle by the political parties and the different sections of the community. Therefore, if they did not have a long period of tutoring, it was only natural that there would be certain expressions of enthusiasm, if we may put it that way – and I challenge any honourable member here to tell me that I am wrong – and it was seen that there was no allegation of fraud or of financial irregularity.

Mr Deputy Speaker, there was neither riot, nor civil commotion.

But certain entrenched, vested interests – and I am not now referring to Bookers-McConnell Limited, because it now appears that they are the most enlightened apostles of the constitution in British Guiana and are carrying the banner way in front of the Premier of British Guiana himself in the advancement towards socialism of some kind or another, whether Eastern or Western, I am not sure yet. They are carrying the banner for reasons which I have not had sufficient time to analyse, but it is a very happy augury for British Guiana that we find the entrenched interests now being prepared to carry the banner of socialism in advance of the political party itself. In October 1953 no indictment was made against the leaders of the government of British Guiana on the grounds that there had been any financial irregularity or anything like that. There was no riot or civil commotion.

The constitution of British Guiana was taken away. The other difference is that we were assured by the then Secretary of State for the Colonies that he did this after consultation with the leader of the government of Barbados, Sir Grantley Adams; the leader of the government of Jamaica, Sir Alexander Bustamente; the leader of the government of Trinidad, Mr Albert Gomes; and he also added the rider that he had even called up the leader of the opposition of Jamaica, Mr Norman Manley. The impression given by the Secretary of State was that all of these leaders had not only approved, but some of them had heralded him and even urged the British government to take away the constitution from the people of British Guiana. Are we, therefore, suprised now that these architects to the destruction of the constitutional rights of the people of British Guiana, that these people who found themselves as leaders of the Westindian embryonic nation, that these people as soon as birth was given to the Westindian nation, decided to strangle it in its birth? How can we be surprised when they strangled the constitution of the people of British Guiana after it was only given to those people six months previously?

Members of this Honourable House must be abundantly clear about the principles involved in the passing of a resolution of this kind. Mr Deputy Speaker, when the constitution of British Guiana was taken away, I along with some other members of the then government, backbenchers as we were at the time in this Chamber, gave expression to our disgust over the action taken by the British government. I remember saying on more than one occasion – and some honourable members who are not fitted with short memories will remember that I said, echoing the words of Mr Edmund Burke in the House of Commons – you will forgive me if I consult my historical encyclopaedia – that in 1780 when Mr Burke was protesting against the action of the British government in the United States, the then American colonies, what he said was that you cannot draw up an indictment against the whole nation. If I had chosen a theme here today as the theme of this Resolution, I would borrow the words of Mr Burke and say: you cannot draw up an indictment against a whole nation.

Sir, what I said on the floor of the House of Assembly in 1954 and 1955 and subsequently was that if an individual minister of the United Kingdom officially expressed adoration for those little things which he knew and things such as hegemony which he knows little about, if he expressed admiration for forms of government over which he had no opportunity to exercise any authority, if this was seditious or illegal, the good Lord in Heaven knows that the laws under the British constitution are so watertight that sometimes if you did not stand up quickly when they played God Save the Queen, you may be hauled into the court and charged with sedition. No one can deny that.

But my attitude was that the laws of the constitution should not be revoked if there were any seditious practices or something which is called seditious libel in the laws of British Guiana, Barbados, Trinidad and other Westindian colonies. Not only seditions, but actions are noticeable; even painting Queen Victoria's statue with red paint, as I understand, was done in British Guiana was noticeable – and even the statue of Lord Willoughby. All of that can be construed to be seditious and you would not have much trouble in getting an indictment under the colonial statues under which we are suffering. But my contention is that if you are guilty of an action which was susceptible of public prosecution before a Court of Law, it is not only right but it is the duty of the members of the Attorney General's Department, and it is the duty of the officer administering the government of the island or the territory, as the case may be, to invite such public prosecution in order to bring the person to boot. The purpose of my saying that is that I think it is grossly unfair that if some little school teacher in Berbice, who one day hopes to be a lawyer and is burning the midnight oil reading constitutional law, exercises his right to choose whom he wants to represent him, somebody should sit down in England and on the advice of a certain administrator take away from him his right to choose the person he wants to preside over his rights.

That is why I echo the words of Mr Edmund Burke. No one has devised a way of drawing up an indictment against a whole nation. Adolf Hitler was the only person who did it, but the way in which he did it was to sign the death warrant of six million people without an indictment at all. The next step to taking away a constitution is to exercise that kind of authoritative function which Adolf Hitler and other dictators exercised.

Sir, you will understand why I say, if the people of British Guiana had done something, then you would have been justified. If the people had taken arms against the sea of troubles which we call the Colonial Office – those are troubles at sea – if the people of British Guiana had made dykes and prevented a landing of British troops or businessmen or had expropriated property of the Crown or done anything of that kind, perhaps you then would have investigated the drawing up of an indictment against the whole people or you would be justified on the banner of public opinion in the taking away of the constitution from the colony.

We would have mismanagement in these islands of ours. In the United Kingdom, a sum of STG£2,000 million was voted between 1935 and 1940 for armaments to protect Great Britain, and when the British Army was confronted by the forces of the enemy at Dunkirk, apart from about three squadrons of the Air Force, and the small pond boats which pushed out from the east coast, they hardly had parasols to hold over their heads because that money was misspent. Up to now that money has not been accounted for. I want to make that clear. I invite you to read your history. Such things do not percolate down to the colonial press, but they send out pictures of the Queen shaking some old lady's hand.

Mr Deputy Speaker, between 1947 and 1958, when the Federation came into being, we witnessed in this Federation, with the active benevolence of the United Kingdom government, a seduction of British Honduras and the rape of the constitution of British Guiana.

In that period both of these (states), through their elected representatives and heads of government had expressed a willingness to join the Westindies Federation. The Rance Report was published in January 1948 – I am speaking purely from memory. In 1953, in the Legislative Council of British Guiana, Dr (Cheddi) Jagan was the only member to vote in favour of the federation. Those leaders I have mentioned did nothing to encourage Mr Richardson or Dr Jagan who became Chief Minister of British Guiana; they did nothing to assist them to make their countries available to the people of the Westindies, but they connived not only at the taking away of the constitution of British Guiana, but they actually assisted to make sure that the Westindian nation was starting off as a puny infant without these territories in which to settle their people or to assist the people of these territories to develop. I say that the doom of the Westindies was sealed when those leaders decided to take away the constitution; but, of course, Dr Jagan is now in complete control of British Guiana. To take away the constitution from British Guiana is to take away the constitution from the electors; you take away the constitution from the people who have the right to vote because you do not give them the right to say how they want their country to be managed when you take away the constitution. I was privileged to witness within a couple of years the same British government under the same political party give back the constitution to the same country of British Guiana.

I was further privileged to witness that, in this year of grace, 1962, a lot of people not necessarily including myself, but not necessarily excluding myself either, you have fought and you have had bloodshed, civil commotion, and a clear expression of the tendency of the government in power to go against the wishes of the people; there was greater justification then for suspending the constitution, even if temporarily, of British Guiana. But the same Conservative government in Britain sent in British troops by plane at the expense of the British taxpayers to shut down the constitution. Just imagine that when the leaders do something, you do not punish the leader, but you take away the constitution of the people. Can you blame any member of the government of Barbados if we do not repose any kind of confidence whatsoever in the discretion of the United Kingdom government which appears to be so preoccupied with the defence of liberalism that they did not have any attention to pay to what they were doing in these areas? As a matter of fact, they have reached the stage of being so demoralised that they want to let go of these colonies like some kind of hot potato, but they want to squeeze out all the pulp before they let them go. That is how it appears to me.

Mr Deputy Speaker, the constitution has been taken away from the people of Grenada by an arbitrary act of the United Kingdom government. What is more deplorable to us in Barbados as a government of the people of this island, is that within twelve months, the United Kingdom government, the same government which we now have re-enfranchising the leader of the Grenada government, in the same manner they have overruled the judgement of a Judge of the Supreme Court in St Lucia. You must ask if we must have any respect for their pronouncements on democratic procedures.

In the neighbouring colony of St Lucia, a Judge of the Supreme Court ruled that there was a breach of the election law and that certain ministers would have to forfeit their seats because of that

40

breach. There is no law which is passed in any of the Windward or Leeward Islands which does not have to be approved by the United Kingdom government. Their election law is actually sent down, like the Decalogue from Mount Sinai, from Church Street. It is not as it is in Barbados where any private member can pass a Bill, and if we do not scrutinise it carefully, we have to abide by the consequences which follow; there are only certain Bills which are reserved for the Royal Assent or Signification; there are very few of them. A law like the awarding of the Princess Alice Scholarship, as the honourable senior member for the City would know, has got to be reserved for Royal Signification; but all the Bills which deal with the constitution of the island, we can decide to pass and make a lot of mistakes; but it is not so in the Leeward and Windward Islands. These Ordinances are sent down from the United Kingdom. Under that law in St Lucia certain Ministers had to forfeit their seats; but because they had somebody in Trinidad, in the Federal Government whom they could not do anything to offend, because the Deputy Prime Minister of the Federation was a St Lucian who rejoices under the name of Dr LaCorbineire, they turned the whole law upside down. Despite what Justice Chenery found – Barbados always seems to be on the wrong end of the stick; we seem always to have Barbadians involved in these things. Mr Justice Chenery ruled that the Ministers should lose their seats; and the Colonial Office said that, despite anything which Mr Justice Chenery did, despite anything which he may have ruled in a Court of Law – and it could not be challenged – the Ministers can still be Ministers. In those circumstances, can we repose any faith in those people? They are playing the game of politics strictly by ear all the time; they have not settled their policy on anything. Those of us who have been following what is taking place in St Lucia, in British Guiana, or in Grenada – well, I cannot say that it came as a surprise to me.

I cannot pretend it is anything that has surprised me, because last week the Secretary of State said he did not like this kind of thing that was going on, and that was five or six days before they actually exercised the Order-in-Council in this matter.

What we regard as being particularly depressing in this matter, Sir, is that we are now trying to build a nation, and by taking arbitrary action of this kind, they are focusing some strictures which are already levelled at the Caribbean area as a whole. We had Mr Castro in Cuba, Sir Grantley Adams in Trinidad, and Mr Jagan in British Guiana, and now they say we have Mr Gairy in Grenada, giving the impression that the Caribbean area, because of the failures and lack of appreciation for the finer points of democracy by some of the people, if not all of them, that I have mentioned, is an area which is always seething, dissatisfied, bordering on Spanish South American Republicanism, and an area in which no one should repose any kind of confidence, because of the gymnastics of a few irresponsible people, and people who, every time they open their mouths, are prone to put both of their feet in them. They now want to project an image as they always do unconsciously, due to their ignorance of the real aspirations of the people of the Westindies, and the real solid basis of Westindian advancement, something which is based on the struggles of the masses of the Westindies, and not on the political leadership of the Westindies. I want to make it clear, and that goes also for this or any other government in Barbados, that any advancement which we have attained has been due to the demonstration of the submerged tenths of the populations and not anything that a leader has condescended to give to the people of the Westindies.

Mr Deputy Speaker, you will always find a leader; and a lot of these governments have been crisis governments. Their political parties have been crisis organisations; they have never had any sound basis either from a business point of view or from a political point of view. There have always been crisis organisations in the Westindies. The idea is: We are having a federal election; so let us get together, although we are not birds of a feather; that is to say, we belong to certain political parties. That is the kind of theory that gave rise to the Bolshevik group in the Soviet Union. We are not really birds of a feather; we are of different plumage; we are, as one member of the opposition has said, blackbirds, among the pigeons all over the place.

I have no hesitation in moving any vote of censure against a Conservative government in England, because I am not a socialist in Barbados, and like some ex-honourable friends of mine who, by the time they get to Canada or the United Kingdom, say that the people in Barbados accuse them of being conservatives, and they are really more conservative than the leaders of the Conservative governments in these countries. When I go to England, I ask them if they know to whom they are talking and tell them they are talking to people who, in the days when police used to be armed with bayonets and bullets, stood up for the masses of these countries.

When Mr Gairy went to Grenada there was a political vacuum. The middle-class people in Grenada had abdicated their right to leadership by ignoring the sufferings of the people of St George's. It is in that kind of atmosphere, where people do not recognise their political responsibilities and their responsibility to the community, that you get dictators and people who are perhaps not fully ripe for leadership issues.

If it is the same people who inspired the British government to think that they can treat the representatives of Grenada with disdain and contempt and to go one step further and take away the constitution not only from the representatives, but from the people of Grenada, then I say that it is time when we must raise a protest; and even although the same people who abdicated their right to leadership by ignoring the masses are the people from whom the constitution has been taken away, I say it serves some of them right, because they are too anxious to play a single game.

A lot of people, Mr Deputy Speaker, accuse me of talking the same way now that I am in government, as if I am still in opposition. They say that I do not remember that I am in government. I did not know that you had to change your tone when you got into government, or that the same tonic *sol-fa* which you had been singing, you had to change to sing some other kind of *oratorio*. I do not understand that at all. I thought that the people had put us on this side because they liked the way we were talking, because of the things which we wanted to do, and the harshest criticism which we can get is that we are still in the opposition. We will be in the opposition until we get the things which we want done, and stop those things which we say that we do not want to be done against the people of the Westindies and the people of Barabdos.

Mr Edwin Burke said: 'I do not know of any method of drawing up an indictment against a whole people.' I say that I do not know of any method of drawing up an indictment against the people of Grenada, and nowhere in the report which was released on the 6th June, 1962, do I find that the commissioners had any indictment to make against the people of Grenada. It is in that sense and spirit and those phrases underlined in this Resolution that I move that this Resolution do now pass.

Federation and the democratic way of life

Statement to Parliament on 20 June, 1962 introducing a resolution to approve the report of the Eastern Caribbean Federation Conference

Mr Deputy Speaker, it is now my privilege to move the passing of this Resolution to approve the Report of the East Caribbean Federation Conference, 1962. It is not necessary for me to go into the history of the development which led up to the dissolution of the Westindian Federation on the 31st of May, 1962. The document which we have before us does not attempt to set out a detailed history of the developments leading up to the establishment and the dissolution of the Westindian Federation. There are certain significant dates which every school child in the Westindies should learn and should know about, and I think that these significant dates would be briefly repeated during the course of a debate of this nature.

In 1947, at the invitation of the then Secretary of State for the Colonies, Mr Creech Jones, delegates from this House and from other Legislatures throughout the British Caribbean area from British Honduras in the north to British Guiana in the south, met in conference; some of the delegates from this Honourable House are still members of this House, and others, although still alive, have gone to other countries, and retired from politics. This Conference took place in 1947 and it was agreed to set up a Standing Closer Association Committee under the Chairmanship of Sir Hubert Rance who was Governor of Trinidad and its dependent territory, Tobago. Perhaps, Mr Deputy Speaker, you will allow me to do something which honourable members of the Legislatures of these islands have appeared to be reluctant to do.

Perhaps you will permit me to acknowledge a debt which they were unprepared to admit, and that is the debt to those Westindians in the United States of America who contributed a substantial amount of money in order to make it possible for the Standing Closer Association Conference to be held in Montego Bay (Jamaica) in 1947.

The Colonial Office – or the British government – is often accused of forcing the Westindies to federate. Personally, it is a view which I do not entirely share, because on an examination of the history and the development of the Federation, you will find that the Colonial Office and the British government were as uncertain about the establishment of a Federation as they have exhibited those uncertainties today in the granting of independence to the East Caribbean, and the shape of a Federation for the East Caribbean. The Secretary of State for the Colonies in 1947, Mr Creech Jones himself, was a Federationist. It is very doubtful whether any of the Caribbean leaders of that day had given the serious examination attendant upon the establishment of a Federation; and the fruit of that has been the result of a total unpreparedness for leadership, a total lack of knowledge of the intricacies of statesmanship demanded of a federal Government. But there is one group of Westindians, quite apart from the students who were studying in the United States of America, Canada and the United Kingdom. This group of persons existed in the areas of New York, Boston, and Chicago; those persons had been brought together by the events in the Westindies of 1937* and have stuck together right through the dim period of the Second World War, taking a very active interest in every political development in the British Caribbean area and, indeed, in a wider context, in the Caribbean as a whole.

It was a result of the efforts which they made, and by the contributions which they made to the cause of Westindian nationhood, that that conference was the success it was in 1947, and indeed it was due to their efforts that the conference was held at all. Westindian governments at that time had not got it into their heads that it was the duty of these governments to take the initiative in matters of constitutional advancement. They were always waiting for leadership from the United Kingdom. Every effort made by political parties in the Westindies up to 1937 had been condemned as being seditious, racial or rebellious and it was up to our American cousins to teach us to clear the mat.

Mr Deputy Speaker, when the history of the Westindies is written, despite our long association with the British Commonwealth of Nations, it will be realised that there was a long, dark period of Westindian history between the end of the First World War and the beginning of the Second World War when there was absolutely no economic assistance of any kind flowing from the United Kingdom in this direction, and when the Westindies' economies were sustained to a very large extent – almost entirely, I should say – by the

*This refers to a series of popular rebellions in several Westindian countries, including Barbados.

remittances which relatives of Westindians resident in the area received from those abroad. First, the Westindians went to build the Panama Canal. From Panama, just about the beginning of the First World War, they moved on to Cuba, and from Cuba they moved to the United States.

Mr Deputy Speaker, that wave of migration did not come to a halt on the introduction of the restrictive Immigration Ordinances by the government of the United States. It continued almost unabated until the time of the depression between the year 1929 and the year 1934 when the flow began to ebb and began to move almost in the opposite direction, because of the vast number of unemployed people there were in the United States and in other countries.

From 1934 until 1937, therefore, we had a period of political and economic stagnation in this island. There were attempts by a few brave souls to enlighten the masses, but the majority of the people who should have been giving leadership to the masses of the Westindies, were content to sit back and do their duty in that state of life to which it had pleased the Almighty to call them, pay no attention to what was going on around them, and accept the status quo as being a pre-ordained and natural state of affairs.

I have always held the theory, Mr Deputy Speaker, that any progress which has come in this Caribbean area, has always been the result of the spontaneous expression of disgust with a situation by the masses, popularly called the 'submerged tenth' of the population of this island. Unfortunately for those who consider government as a natural preserve for one stratum of society, the submerged tenth is now emerging as nine-tenths of the population and not one-tenth at all. No Alexander Hamilton has risen. There has never been the need perhaps for a George Washington as the General of a Westindian army. It has always been the movement of people within and without the territory which brought into focus the very dire economic conditions under which the majority of the people in these islands suffered.

The Panama Canal was built substantially by the toil and sweat of Westindian labour. But it was the income which the workers on the Panama Project managed to earn between the seven years immediately preceding the First World War which prevented the people of these islands from demonstrating, in rebellious manner, their disgust against the conditions under which they were supposed to exist.

Then during the First World War, large numbers of Westindians rallied to the Flag. I think that the British government ought to be reminded of this sometimes, because when we see the craven way in which the British government is today crawling at the feet of their oppressors, the people who tried to destroy the British Commonwealth of Nations on at least two occasions in a quarter of a century, and when we look at the disdain and the contempt with which they are prone to treat peoples whom Rudyard Kipling described as the lesser members without the law, and in the words of the hymnist, the people who inhabit the countries where the heathen in his blindness is supposed to bow down to wood and stone, when we regard all of these things on one side and look at the almost childish loyalty of the Westindian masses on the other, the way in which they rallied to defend what Mr Churchill said is the bastion of freedom on more than one occasion in twenty-five years, I do not see how anyone who has the honour of participating in the administration of these areas can be so much out of his mind as to deprive the people of their constitutional rights.

Westindians were not reluctant in answering the call, whether in the armed services or in factories or on the beaches. The Westindians, the Barbadians, St Lucians, Antiguans could be found whether in the steaming jungle of Malaya or in the cold regions of the North Atlantic on convoy patrols, on the upper deck welding steel ships which the Americans so graciously made available to the British Merchant Shipping Service; wherever the conflict was being waged the Westindians were there. Not a single Westindian has ever been impeached for selling secrets to the enemy, for any disloyalty to the Flag or doing any of those things which would be inimical to the successful prosecution of a war.

I am not going back 150 years or 200 years to talk about the blood and the sweat, to talk as Dr (Eric) Williams has done in his famous treatise about 'Capitalism and Slavery', to show how the industrial wealth of Great Britain was financed by the unfree labour of the workers of the Westindies; those are matters which are accepted by the most rabid, reactionary Conservative in Great Britain, and there is absolutely no point in our re-emphasising the industrial debt which the industrialists owe to the ancestors of the people of the Westindies. It does not get us anywhere. That is as true of John 3:16. That was never a matter for argument; and if the Premier of that territory of Trinidad and Tobago has made any contribution to the economic history of mankind, it is in underlining and documenting the foundation on which that industrial development has been built up.

During the dark days of the depression, during the inter-war period, the period of stagnation, there were no development and welfare organisations, there was no economic policy, no Colombo

Plan. Many of these things we in the Westindies are still without and bereft of. We were just regarded as geographical areas to which school masters in the United Kingdom could say that the sun never sets on the British Empire. The Westindies, apart from the cricket field, first came into prominence because the ordinary men and women in the street, and not any political leader, decided to revolt and rebel against those conditions, although they were not revolting against any individuals or any countries. In 1937, they called them disturbances. In another country, they would call them insurgents, revolutionaries or rebels because the jargon of nationalism is very often qualified by the impression which the person who is being protested against wants to give to the rest of the world.

Out of that rebellion, out of all that social protest, came the appointment of the Royal Commission of very highly qualified persons of integrity in the public life of the United Kingdom who published a very forthright report on the conditions which they found in the Westindies and who recommended that the economic salvation of the Westindies lay along the road to Federation; and the Montego Bay Conference, coming as it did nearly two years after the end of the Second World War, was the first direct recognition that the recommendations of the Royal Commission should be implemented.

The Standing Closer Association Committee met frequently in the territory of Trinidad under the chairmanship of Sir Hubert Rance and published a report in 1948 which lay on the shelf of the Westindian Legislatures for a very long time. It was not until some time in the 50s, around 1952 and 1953, that the Legislatures, including the Barbados House of Assembly, got around to the job of even discussing the Standing Closer Association Committee's report which had been published some years before; and it is symbolic of the attitude of the Westindian leaders of that era that they had to wait for a directive from the Secretary of State for the Colonies before they had the courage to present the idea of a Federation of the peoples of these territories.

I had the privilege along with at least 40 per cent of the honourable members whom I can see around this horseshoe table in this Assembly of making some kind of contribution to the debate which took place on the Standing Closer Association Committee's Report.

There was not a single dissenting voice at that time and I hope that, by the time we conclude the discussion on the report which I now hold in my hand, there will be some measure of unanimity for the necessity – rather, the plausibility – for Barbados to join the Association with our brethren across the seas; we will be setting the clock back if, at this stage of our development, we are going to stop and hesitate and wonder what are the advantages to be derived from an association of this kind.

If the Westindian leaders who jumped into the Federation when it was clear that there was a certain amount of status for them, and that certain Imperial honours would be attendant upon being recognised as a larger area – if they had done their job to educate the people of the Westindies in the exercise of a Federal Constitution, there would not be any need for my discourse this afternoon.

The government does not intend to steamroller or stampede through with this discussion. We are going to give everybody, even the slow-witted, sufficient time to read, mark, learn and inwardly digest the contents of this document, because once we put our hands to the plough there cannot be any turning back this time. We have to plough a very straight furrow which will have no bends or crookedness.

Mr Deputy Speaker, there are a lot of mealy-mouthed politicians and people in the newspaper world who only believe in indulging in cheap sensationalism, and who believe there is a thing called the freedom of the Press. I do not know whether you went to some legal institution where they were able to tell you what this mysterious freedom of the Press is supposed to be; but as far as I know, there is no such thing as the freedom of the Press. The Press does not enjoy any more freedom than any other citizen in this country. The Press has the same right to criticise anyone, the same right to use their own property in a way which does not interfere with the proprietary rights of their neighbours, the same right to say things provided they fall short of the laws of libel and defamation; but the Press does not enjoy any special status or any special freedom. The Press, however, has a responsibility, a responsibility which they do not always appear to be conscious of; and when they indulge in exercises of this kind, and allow even correspondents in the Readers Columns to write disparaging articles about the Westindian people, and to write poems about 'Ten Little Countries', they are only concealing their contempt like Agatha Christie when she wrote a book about 'Ten Little Nigger Boys'.

A Press which allows advertisements to appear stating that only people of a certain racial origin need apply for certain jobs is not exercising freedom; that Press is abdicating its responsibility and duty to the people of the country where that Press is making a profit for its Directors. In this Year of Grace, 1962, we want someone to write a National Anthem; we do not want clever correspondents doing like

Agatha Christie and writing about 'Ten Little Nigger Boys'. I want to tell them that there are eight countries and not any 'Little Eight', and these eight territories, despite anything that may happen, are not falling off any wall, because if there was anything we decided in London as presented in this Report on the Federation Conference of 1962, we have decided to build a monument more lasting than bronze and certainly more lasting than that erected by the late architects of the destruction of the Westindian nation.

Anyone who does not understand the economic, political and geographical background of the Westindies will not readily appreciate why these islands should want to come together in a federal system of government. If there were one area which a federal system of government eminently suits, it is the Eastern Caribbean.

There has been little communication culturally between one island and another but when you look at the broad masses of people in the Westindies, they do have a common affinity, although in individual islands they have their own way of looking at things. We are, therefore, bound together by some ties of consanguinity, it is true, but we are bound together by similar conditions and similar economic background more than anything else. We are bound together because we believe that most of us were displaced from some part of Africa, some may have come from Dahomey, some from Uganda, some from Gambia, some from the Ebou nation, some from Mozambique, some from Dakar, and from all parts of the continent our ancestors may have been brought against their wishes. But when you look at a country like Barbados and you realise that the average Barbadian is completely detribalised and has more cultural standing and is allied more closely to those people in western industrial nations, one cannot really go on with that nebulous affinity in order to prove we have a common destiny. It may have been established that we have a common past, but we have been bound together by historical and physical accidents, because we have looked to one metropolitan country for control and leadership, and because the pattern of jurisprudence, the pattern of constitutional institutions and parliamentary institutions which we have followed all along has been the pattern which has been given to us by the government of the United Kingdom. Therefore, having one system now of parliamentary democracy (we) are bound together by a common respect of law, and being still in a relatively low state of economic advancement, we now aspire under these common bonds, however slender they are, to weld ourselves together in a nation in which each man would have his self-respect and so that we can assist each other in uplifting the standard of living for the people of the area.

The First Barbados Budget (Abridged)

First financial statement and budget proposals, delivered in Parliament on 26 June, 1962*

I promised honourable members of this honourable House that before the end of June 1962, I would be introducing the real budget proposals and the Development Plan of this government. It is in keeping with that promise that I rise today to make this Financial Statement. One honourable member has referred to the fact that there has never been this procedure before; that is not very difficult to understand because there has never been a budget. What happened in the past is that the Leader of the House or the Premier brought in a conglomeration of statistics which glorified in the name of Colonial Estimates, and in the course of disgorging a mass of statistics he would, in passing, mention that certain fiscal measures would be carried out. I was never in charge of the finance and indeed there was no Minister of Finance.

Mr Deputy Speaker, this island of Barbados is to a large degree dependent on external trade, on the amount of money which tourists are able to spend in the island, and on the remittances which we obtain from relatives, friends and well-wishers abroad. This is not a manufacturing economy wherein the people consume the product of industry, and where we get a turnaround of the money in the country entirely independent of external trade.

The proposals which I intend to make, therefore, must be read in

* (Errol W Barrow was the first Finance Minister of Barbados, serving in this capacity for 15 unbroken years from 1961, until his Democratic Labour Party – DLP – was voted out of office in 1976.

He turned over the Finance portfolio to Dr Richard C Haynes when the DLP was returned to office in May 1986, but kept a close oversight on the country's finances as Minister of Economic Affairs.

Dr Haynes resigned three months after Mr Barrow died, complaining of a breakdown of communications between himself and the new Prime Minister, Mr L. Erskine Sandford.

Mr Barrow intoduced the annual Financial Statement and Budget Proposals with the above presentation in 1962. Today, 25 years later, the format for this exercise remains largely unchanged).

the context of the peculiar nature of our economy. I propose to deal with the economic developments in this island and outside which have bearing on our position today. When we look at the world economic position in the light of our own circumstances, we find that the major problem is a shortage of capital, a shortage of money which emerging countries and highly developed countries all need in order to increase their national incomes by way of investment. This shortage of capital has made itself felt in no uncertain way on the economies of the Caribbean area, because we look primarily to the United Kingdom as a source of our investment capital. At the present moment the trend is for short term investment, thereby accentuating the shortage which already exists. Not only do we find that private institutions, private companies and public companies and private manufacturers are indulging in this exercise of short term investment and short term borrowing, but it is a marked feature of the United Kingdom economy today. Everything today is very much in a state of flux, and it is only natural that the people who have the propensity to save, the people who accumulate surplus will much sooner invest in a short term security than in a long term one. This new feature is most attractive to would-be investors, because the average person who has this amount of capital, or a certain amount of capital to invest, would much sooner know he is going to get back all his capital in two years' time with the opportunity to reinvest if conditions are changing as rapidly as we have seen them change, than to invest in Government securities.

Mr Deputy Speaker, not only do we find in the public sector that this trend is now becoming the order of the day, but private industrialists, private entrepreneurs and private businessmen themselves are offering short term borrowing at very attractive rates of interest which makes it all the more difficult for people in our position. The next factor which I think has made its influence felt on the economic position of these islands in particular, is the proposal of the United Kingdom to venture into the European Common Market. The British government, as you know, Sir, has been negotiating for a long period – I think perhaps over twelve months – with the Inner Six in Europe over the conditions under which Great Britain will be permitted to enter the European Economic Community. The effect on us is that these negotiations have generated an atmosphere of uncertainty over the future of the colonies. British investors, therefore, are looking more towards the East in the direction of the Common Market countries than to the overseas territories, as places where investment should take place.

The third factor, Sir, is the uncertainty of the movements, political and economic, in the area in which we live. It is most unfortunate that quite a large number of people in the United Kingdom, in Canada, and in the United States of America are completely ignorant about the geographical and political facts of life in the Caribbean area. This lack of knowledge on their part is due mainly to the distance which separates us from them and because our economic plight and our political situation do not enter in their day-to-day thinking, or make any impact on their standard of living from time to time. The Westindian area is a very small microcosm in the language of international trade. More recently and closer to us, there have been unfavourable movements in the United States money markets.

The average price of investments has fallen to new lows at least twice during the past six weeks. The uncertainty of the investment atmosphere in the United States and in England must, therefore, reflect on the possibilities of these territories being able to urge the necessity for immediate investment capital in the region as a whole.

The fourth factor, Mr Deputy Speaker, has been the chronic over-production of sugar in the world. Sugar being our main export from Barbados, when we get over-production, although we have a guaranteed price under the Commonwealth Sugar Agreement for a substantial amount of the sugar which we produce, yet we have had to sell a considerable amount of that sugar at the World Market Price, and this year it would probably be in the vicinity of ten or twelve thousand tons at World Market Price under the Commonwealth Sugar Agreement. Indeed, this year, the World Market Price is less than half of the negotiated price and, therefore, the small producer, the peasant in Barbados, is very often adversely affected by World Market Price, although he was not aware of it.

Our production this year has fallen well below the estimates of the experts and the planters of Barbados, although there were some planters who were very pessimistic when everyone was calculating on a very good crop indeed. However, the revised figures for sugar production this year are 159,000 tons. This fall in production is largely attributed to the poor quality of the juice, to the pests and parasites who alone in the Westindies are learning to dwell together in unity.

We now come to tourism. This year 1961 was a record year when 37,060 tourists came to the island. In the first quarter of 1962, 12,323 tourists arrived as compared with 10,750 in the first quarter of last year.

When we come to our trade outlook and our trade figures for the past year, our imports were in value $80,281,000. We exported

$43,177,000 in value leaving a trade gap of $37,104,000.

The value of our imports of food alone was more than $23 million. The value of our manufactured goods was $20 million; the value of machinery and transport equipment was $12 million. I do estimate that the amount of the adverse trade balance in 1961 was covered by our net invisible credits; such matters as our income from tourism, our dividends and interest payments from abroad and remittances from our dependents – or should I say our supporters because we are the dependents – our friends, and relatives in the United Kingdom and the United States.

If I may now turn to the population figures. At the end of last year, the population was estimated to have been 241,655, rather less than the previous year's figure of 242,274. The natural increase of 4,344 was covered by our net migration of 4,493. In the first quarter of 1962, 173 more people have come to the island than have left. This may be due to the fact of the United Kingdom Emigration Act which comes into force in about a week's time. At the end of 1961 there were 131,922 females in this island and 109,733 males; in other words, 22,187 more females than males in Barbados. I do not know whether we should advertise this to attract more people from the other islands, but I wish it will rejoice the hearts of some of the honourable members in this Chamber.

The index of retail prices rose by 1.7 points, one per cent between March 1961 and March 1962. That would seem to compare itself with some of the wage increases of the magnitude of 35 per cent and 38 per cent which were recently given to some of our workers in this country, and, therefore, one will see quite readily that there will be quite a lot to cushion the shock of some of the proposals which I intend to make. The wage increases have imposed a great strain on the resources of the island. In other words, they have reduced the amount of employment which could be provided. I think that that will be obvious to everyone.

At the 31st March, 1962, loans and advances by commercial banks totalled $44,475,000 while deposits were $44,246,000. Of these deposits, $20,551,000 represent savings deposits; As to current expenditure, the actual amount was $27,219,000; the revenue was $26,515,000. The deficit on current account, therefore is $1,004,000. We have estimated this year, of course, for a deficit of over $2.3 million.

As far as capital expenditure last year is concerned, the total amount of capital expenditure in the island by government was $6,732,000.

Mr Deputy Speaker, the issue of Treasury Bills, the primary object of which is to assist in the promotion of a local securities market, is proceeding slowly but satisfactorily.

I will now go on to give the Treasury prospects for the year 1962-63. Although the crop has been smaller than expected, I do not wish at this stage to revise the approved Estimates of Revenue and Current Expenditure for the year 1962-63. The Customs Revenue will to a great extent be dependent on the expectations for next year's crop and the next tourist season and the income tax yield will reflect the profits of last year. In the Approved Estimates for 1962-63 the Revenue is estimated at $25,543,778; the estimated expenditure was $26,895,967, leaving an excess over revenue, or what we call in normal language, a budget deficit of $2,352,189. This is the background, Sir, against which my fiscal proposals will relate.

I now turn to the economic prospects for the year 1962-63. I have already mentioned the world position and our inter-dependence for the advice of international trade. I should also mention that the United States of America is becoming of great importance to the economy of this island. You will remember, Sir, that the Secretary of State issued a statement about three months ago over our proposals for federation of the Windward and Leeward Islands and Barbados and said in that statement quite bluntly that these islands, no doubt because of Great Britain's proposed entry into the European Economic Community, would have to look more and more to the United States and other countries for economic assistance and technical assistance.

Another aspect of the economies of these islands – and when I mention the area as a whole, it is because we cannot exist in a vacuum here in Barbados – is the aspect of confidence which people must have in the area. This is the most important question in all financial matters. It is true that a large degree of the lack of confidence exhibited sometimes is due to the lack of knowledge, or, if I may put it in blunt English, the ignorance of the people in the metropolitan countries about the facts of life in these areas. But we also have to admit that a lack of confidence sometimes is induced by the behaviour of our people inside the area and by people who should know better. It is induced by irresponsible writings and statements and by irresponsible actions on the part of our politicians.

I think that we in the Westindies should not be afraid to speak our minds. I think that we in the Westindies should not be looking around for somebody else to lead and work out our own political and economic philosophy and I do not think that it pays any Westindian politician either to look too rapidly in the direction of European or Asiatic countries for our basic philosophies of life. We have to work out the way of life which is congenial to the people who live in these islands, and we have to act in a responsible manner without, of course, losing our self-respect and grumbling to people who should be on the same terms as ourselves.

The basic situation, however, financially speaking, is not unfavourable. As far as Barbados is concerned, in our economic prospects for 1962-63, the weather has given us a good start for our sugar crop; the tourist trade is expanding; but we must always bear in mind our inter-dependence on international conditions, and recession even in the Dominion of Canada or in the United States of America would adversely affect our tourist prospects for the current year.

The trade with the Windward and Leeward Islands is small in comparison with our total trade – our visible trade – but nevertheless it is a valuable trade for us.

We need in the context of limited migration, in the context of necessity for capital investment and to pay the interest charges which will necessarily be attendant upon the borrowing of money from abroad or locally – the greatest need, therefore, is to find productive employmnet for our increasing population. If I could sum up the government's attitude towards the general economic position in three words – Your Honour will forgive me if I am a little political – I say that our programme must be for discipline, loans and production: it must be the D.L.P.** on other words.

I now come to the discipline. As I told members of my Cabinet an hour before the House began its sitting, you can now fasten your seat belts and prepare for take off. I have considered various methods of raising the large amount of revenue required to meet the increased salaries and wages of government employees and to pay debt charges on the loans which have to be raised to defray the capital expenditure.

I forgot to mention Sir, 'no smoking', but you must still keep your seat belts fastened. My promise not to increase the rates of income tax will be kept, but something must be done about the arrears. At 31st March, 1962, they reached the enormous figure of $1,285,722; that was the amount of taxation owing to the Commissioner of Inland Revenue.

It should be clear that this government is faced today with an exceedingly tough problem, and investigation of the island's finances

** A play on the abbreviation for Barrow's Democratic Labour Party.

56

has shown that if prompt measures are not taken to right the situation, Barbados will either have to go cap in hand to some other country for annual budgetary support or, alternatively, to introduce a drastic reduction in salaries and wages, either one of which will tend to pervert our political and financial outlook. If anyone had doubts as to the determination of this government to put our finances on a very sound basis, he will now realise that he was mistaken. Those who have been studying what has been happening in this island should not be shocked at what I am now about to propose in my first budget. I do not propose to take half measures. It is not just a few additional dollars that are needed from taxation, but between two million dollars and three million dollars per annum, for this year alone.

As much as any other member of the community, being a taxpayer myself – I know that there is a popular myth that politicians do not pay any taxes, but we have to pay our taxes before anybody else – I regret the necessity for these measures.

Land Rights, Conservatism and the Church

Address to Parliament 23 June, 1964 on the acquisition
of land for the establishment of the Cave Hill Campus of
the University of the Westindies (UWI)
(Slightly abridged)

I have been very distressed over the remarks which I have heard
during the short time that I have been listening to the debate. I am
distressed, Sir, very much because of the unkind remarks which were
made against the government to the effect that the government
wanted to expropriate people's property. We are not concerned with
the political parties in Barbados, but with the social philosophy which
should exist in this island. This is a speech which I could have made if
honourable members on the other side of the House were not
interested in personalities, but in principles, at the time when the
Land Acquisition Act was amended by this government.

The Land Acquisition Act, 1949, was amended by this government
for the simple reason that it was our experience that the provisions of
the Act were such that the whole community could be held up to
ransom by recalcitrant land-owners. I may say I am not putting the
gentleman concerned in this particular transaction in that category; I
am not being personal at all. This government has embarked on a
development programme.

The only acquisition not involving compensation which has ever
take place in Barbados, is the 92 acres reclaimed at the Deep Water
Harbour.

We have inherited a social and economic system whereby the large
plantations, or 80 per cent of the plantations, or of the arable land in
Barbados, belongs to 360 people. I am not including the gentleman
with whom the official opposition is so much concerned, he being a
member of their party, I believe.

Let us look at this matter in its right perspective. We have an island
of 166 square miles, and with a population of 240,000. We have an

average of 14,000 people to the square mile and the average Barbadian has no chance of ever holding a sizeable proportion of this island on which he could rear two cows and three pigs. If you win money you can buy land from somebody who wants to dispose of it or you can make use of the Court of Chancery in order to increase your holdings. There are many people who have gone to the United States of America and have helped their grandsons and their aunts and they have come back here and found that their relatives have passed their land through the court and acquired title. Barbadians are land hungry.

We have large numbers of people who cannot afford to buy land at the existing prices; we have people in the lower brackets, who, if this government did not have a policy of providing for housing areas, would not have owned any of this land. The word 'conservatism' just means holding on to what you have at all costs or at a special price to the detriment of everybody else in the community.

In 1794 the conservatives resisted the introduction of income tax as they did later to Mr Gladstone's Reform Bills and the Education Act. Because I speak to conservatives, it does not mean that I accept the philosophy of conservatism. You have a majority who never had any chance of owning anything. That is the kind of situation which is endemic in a community such as this and that leads to much more serious things than acquisition. It leads to what is taking place in British Guiana, that is to say, 53 deaths within a few weeks. You have people owning thousands of acres of land on the one hand, and on the other hand, you have the man who is never in possession of sufficient money, some of which he can save so as to buy shoes for his children; and you cannot persuade him that even those responsible agitators, such as they are in British Guiana, who come along and say: 'look at what this man has, and what the other man has', are not Messiahs.

In all this you make room for the Jagans, the Brindley Benns and the Castros. The philosophy of conservatism is such that it creates that kind of situation, but what we are trying to do in Barbados, is to give the people in this country an opportunity for education, a chance of getting a square meal, a chance of living in a decent house, and a chance of getting a job for which they are qualified, without any discrimination whatever. Those are the things we have been trying to do and we have not created any revolution in this country.

I would not even try to pretend that a social revolution has taken place in this country. All that has taken place in Barbados in the last two years, is that we have managed to satisfy the people in this country that all is not lost and that something can be done to ease their lot, although we cannot guarantee them pie in the sky or mansions in Spain.

Now let us be honest and straightforward about this whole thing. The reason why I am speaking in this debate – and I intend to speak at some length – is because this debate has highlighted the fundamental differences in the social and economic philosophies existing between the major parties in this House, in other words, between the government on the one side, and the official opposition on the other. Therefore, this is a good opportunity to have a restatement of why we think as we think, why we know that we are right, and why we know that if we were not here, the people who have vested interests would be completely oblivious to the low living standards of the rest of the community, completely unconcerned that their indifference has created the gun powder that might actually make them insecure and blow them through the roof.

They themselves create the conditions, and unless you have a group of people in this country who are prepared to redress the imbalances, to see things in the broad, social context, to see the economic importance of legislation, the economic importance of development, the psychological importance of removing distinctions between one class of the community and the other, then you are asking for trouble.

All that those people on the other side are doing this afternoon is inviting trouble, because they do not seem to know how the masses of people think. We have been the safety valve and we are prepared to act as the safety valve, but we must be satisfied that there is some reconditioning going on on the other side, and there is some kind of rethinking and a restatement of their own position being satisfactorily made in their own minds and the people they are supposed to represent.

For this particular small parcel of land which was producing nothing, which has no services, no roads, no light, and no water, in my humble opinion, the price which was offered by the government was generous and far from being absurd as some honourable members would suggest.

Now I want to clear the air on certain fundamental matters. I regard this as a personal debate for this reason – the members of the conservative party are not going to like what I say; as the honourable senior member for St Peter has often said, and I join with him in this.

I am not looking for any friends now that I am in government because I did not have any before and those whom I had, I have clasped them to my bosom with bonds of steel. But I do not waste my time with each new-found, untried comrade. If I get up here, therefore, and have to offend some people in stating what the philosophy of this Party is, it does not worry me, because all the time that these individuals were growing wealthy, they were not with you. When we were fighting the battle of the masses, they were not with us, because after they reach a certain stage, their social ideas and economic philosophies crystallised and not only crystallised, but they coalesced into groups and the more acquisitive they are, the more unconscious they are of the basic needs of a community.

They are all of them extremely acquisitive but we expect this. We are not saying that it is a crime, but in every democratic society, you will find people like this who do not take the trouble to look around the world and see what is happening, and you will always find them adopting this holier than thou attitude, that you are coming to take away what thay have, that you must go and work for it.

Mexico is one of the richest states today, but they were not talking about that in 1923 when the oil fields were taken over. One of the greatest oil-producing countries in the world is Venezuela, but you have about 70 per cent of the population illiterate, and some of the people have to walk miles to the centre of town to get a bucket of water.

Are we going to let people who have been able to amass money come in from outside and when the public programme demands that something should be done, hold up the progress of this community on the basis that somebody can take an aeroplane trip to America and persuade somebody to pay more money than the government is able to pay for a parcel of land? It is as simple as that.

I will tell you something right now, Mr Speaker, even if His Lordship the Bishop may get offended. When I see some of the people who go to the Anglican Church in this island, my infrequency of attendance rises, because I notice that they, like the Republicans in the United States, and the Southern Protestants, are always the most acquisitive people, and if you want to find people who have a little more social philosophy, you have to look for the Baptists or Methodists, because the established church in Barbados has been for generations a church of vested interests. It is a property owner, and, therefore, all the property owners tend to congregate there, and they think it is not respectable to go somewhere else.

I was born, baptised, and confirmed in the Anglican Church, therefore, I speak without any impunity. The infrequency of my attendance at church is because I have noticed that good Protestants are the most acquistive people. So, you will see that we have a religious organisation, buttressing up these people and you will never see in the Anglican Church, anybody being critical of the landed gentry of this country. I have never heard of one Anglican Priest saying that you should have canteens for workers at factories and plantations, but I have heard of ministers, like the late Francis Godson, from other denominations talking of old age pensions for the people.

We are getting more trouble from the people in the Anglican Church over this same question of land, than from anybody else. We are saying this about these pious Anglican politicians going into church so that you should know that there are going there to have a sense of security. You have rectors who want to charge the government more for land than the biggest capitalists in the United States would want to charge their government. Therefore, I have to say these unkindly things but I am speaking facts. I want to be like the late Prime Minister of India – I want my ashes scattered all over the sea thus relieving the City Council of the pressure with which they are now faced of finding more land for a burial place.

The reason I have mentioned the Anglican Church is just because I want to show that its philosophy was so deeply engrained in the sanctity of private property ownership; that it has become glorified in its religion and it has actually been sponsored and promoted by the Anglican Church. As a matter of fact, they want us to pay three million dollars for their property now, when they have kept it for all these years in the state of condition which it is now. Who are their advisers, but the same people that come in here and who write letters to the newspapers talking of the iniquities of socialism?

We realised what the programme of development of this government would be over the next four years, and we introduced a bill to amend the Land Acqusition Act of 1949 because we had been experiencing difficulties, and so as to give a more realistic method of compensating owners without in any way depriving them of the benefit of a reasonable return for their investments. The whole philosophy of conservative capitalism is based on getting a reasonable return for your investment. What is a reasonable return? There is no capitalist who will quarrel with you if you say that you should get a percentage of your money.

In this particular case the land is in the middle of nowhere. The owner ceased to use it even for agricultural purposes three years ago; the land is not even fit for grazing two heads of sheep, and I see people grazing 20 or 30 sheep on a quarter acre of land or even less than that.

However, as far as these 19 acres of land are concerned, you could not find two sheep grazing there between 1950 and 1961. I have never seen any landowners in Barbados give up anything out of which they are making money. Far from that, you cannot show me any land owners, people who were firmly entrenched and have their roots deep, and their tentacles high in the economy of this country, giving up anything by gift or otherwise that they can make money out of.

The average Barbadian has a reputation for being hard working because he has no other alternative. He cannot go out into the forests and carve out an existence for himself like the homesteaders did in the United States of America.

If you were to examine the social and economic structure in this island, you will find that the pattern has not been so radically changed over the past 100 years. Some people have inherited land, some people have won land, some people have been able to speculate and accumulate a little money and buy land and others have used the courts to expropriate the legitimate owners of land, which is a disgrace to any civilised society.

Now we are offering a man £300 an acre for land on which we probably have to spend $50,000 in order to get this land developed, but he is asking $10,000 an acre for land which did not bring any income over the past three years, and which he acquired at a price which is less than one-tenth of what the government is offering him. Where is the justice in this matter?

This government is putting terrific pressure on land owners because we want living space for the people of this island. There are more people who are working now than have ever worked before in the history of this island, and we are not going to allow 360 people who own 80 per cent of the land to exploit the other 230,000.

You only hear about exploitation when somebody's corns are getting crushed. You do not hear about exploitation in other circumstances.There are people who feel that if a man is born in a house 16' x 9' no government is to give him the opportunity of having a little more expansion because he is a man living in a house 16' x 9', while they are the 300-acre men.

Politics is a question of what is the basic philosophy; but some people have not got any philosophy at all. Some of us have basic philosophy and there are people who have a lot of money but no philosophy at all; those are the ones who do not want to hear of anything which challenges the sacred institution of private property. It does not matter how courteous you are; you can drive a man to commit suicide by putting him in a bad financial position and that is regarded as good business ethics; but whenever you have to interfere with the sacred institutions, you hear this talk about robbing a poor man.

"This is the parting of the ways"

Speech in Parliament, introducing a resolution calling on Britain to convene the Barbados Independence Conference, 4 January, 1966

Mr Speaker, there is in the constituency of His Honour the Deputy Speaker, a monument which commemorates the landing of the settlers in Barbados in 1605. People who are more accurate in their historical facts believe that the settlers came to the island from the United Kingdom in the year 1625. This Parliament was first instituted in 1639.

There are many people, even the Editors of Halsbury's Laws of England, who are not fully cognisant of the nature of the relationship which exists between the dependent countries in the Commonwealth and the metropolitan country.

We have in this island, a flexible constitution in the full and truest sense of the term. Unlike the inflexible constitution of the neighbouring country of Trinidad and Tobago and the constitution of the United States of America, our constitution bears similarity only to the constitution of the United Kingdom, in that it is partly founded on convention and usage, and partly contained in written statutes and constitutional documents known to us in this parliament as the Letters Patent and the Royal Instructions.

When the settlers landed in 1625, they brought the laws of the United Kingdom with them; so that all the laws, customs and usages of Parliament were imported into this Chamber on its foundation in 1639. You may wonder, Mr Speaker, why it is necessary for me to make this excursion into the dim recesses of the constitutional history of this island. It is precisely because there are so many people in this island who are unaware of the long, slow process of constitutional evolution of which the Resolution which we are discussing today is the apotheosis that it is necessary for me to have this debate conducted on a level where the people whom we are addressing will understand the premises from which we speak and the premises on which we stand.

When the Parliament convened in 1639 it was convened under the

Lords of the Council of this island – the Lord Lieutenant General of the island, the Lords of the Council and the General Assembly of this island – to make laws for the better government of the territory under a franchise granted by the Sovereign of the United Kingdom. These territories were run as plantations. We have not fully got rid of the plantation mentality. A franchise was granted to Sir William Courteen, the Earl of Carlisle, who appointed as Governor the Eighth Lord Willoughby and, in exchange for this franchise, a certain tribute was exacted by the Imperial Government in the form of taxation which was levied on the people of this country by a process of sub infeudation from the Lord Lieutenant-General himself, on to the lesser, may I call them, barons and on to the lower order of plantation chivalry that existed in those days, if there is chivalry in the plantation system. In the year 1651 – this was a considerable time before the American Declaration of Independence, precisely perhaps 125 years before the famous Declaration in what is now known as the United States of America, by the 13 British Colonies which we have helped to populate and to develop from these shores in Barbados – the Lord in Council and the General Assembly of this island in protest against the Navigation Laws, the same type of Navigation Laws that the 13 Colonies rebelled against 125 years later, they were a bit slower than the people of Barbados, issued their famous Declaration of Independence, not from this Chamber, because as far as I can discover, this Chamber had not been built, but certainly the Lords of the Council and the General Assembly of this island declared themselves an independent nation. The significant thing about this is that I have not been able to discover anywhere in the records of this House that the Unilateral Declaration of Independence which was made in 1651 has ever been repealed by this House or by any other person.

Shortly after this Declaration – General, Sir George Ayscue bombarbed the township of Oistins, and after two days' fighting a long boat was launched with a white flag and a treaty was signed between the people of Barbados and the United Kingdom government at a place called the Mermaid Tavern in the township of Oistins on the southern coast of this island. In that treaty the people of Barbados agreed to pay four-and-a-half per cent in exchange for the repeal of the Navigation Laws vis-a-vis the merchants and colonists of this country. Our relationship, therefore, with Great Britain has never been a 'status' relation from the very early days which existed in places more properly described as Crown Colonies and which achieved internal self-Government only in the 1950s – territories like

Trinidad and Tobago, the Lesser Antilles, Mauritius, and all the other island territories over which Britain held sway.

Right from the beginning and long before some of these territories were discovered or settled, the relationship between the people of this country and the government of the United Kingdom, had been a relationship of contract and not a relationship of status. That is what has probably distinguished Barbados from any other Westindian island. Its approach has always been a contractual approach and not an approach of status. We continued to make laws. You will find the very earliest Act we have on the Statute Books is, as far as I can remember, in 1667, a law against forcible entry into any lands or tenements.

When the restoration of the monarchy took place, recognition was given to the loyalty of Barbados which is now proverbial – and to me sometimes is questionable in the sense that Barbadians hold loyalty to things which they know nothing about. They do not understand their duty of loyalty to their own country under the Constitution, but this loyalty to the British government was acknowledged. This means that this island was treated with a certain amount of deference to the extent that the island has been left to manage its own affairs. Far from the British government either contributing one penny to the support of the general revenue of this island in a direct manner – from that time until today, all the pro-consular officials have been paid by the people of Barbados although they had no say in their nomination. The Chief Secretaries not only have been paid, and continue to be paid, but the people of Barbados also provided them with living accommodation and with luxuries which are not even vouchsafed to Ministers of Government today, although we are responsible for running the government today. All of these things, Barbadians have accepted, as I have said from that day right on to this, the British government has not contributed one penny towards the general revenue of this island.

Other territories, on the other hand, received and are still receiving substantial annual grants-in-aid, not of development, but in aid of administration and to pay the same Pro-consular officers, the same civil servants, and to pay for the keeping of law and order. They are not for the purpose of paying for the carrying out of development programmes and, unless one appreciates that there are territories who have lived on the 'hand-outs' of the Colonial Office from time immemorial and that Barbados has never been in this invidious position, you cannot understand how difficult it is for us in the Westindies to come together under constitutional arrangements.

We in Barbados have never found ourselves in this position where we had to ask for financial aid from what is fondly – and I say 'fondly' advisedly – described as the Mother Country. We have never been in this unhappy situation. As a matter of fact, I can recount where we have contributed towards the revenues of the United Kingdom.

We have a long history of constitutional government which antedates the constitutional history of the United States, which antedates the constitutional history of any of the Westindian territories, which antedates the constitutional history of the South American countries. It should be that when the Leader of the House rises to his feet and says 'Mr Speaker, I beg to move that this Resolution do now pass,' if the Leader of Her Majesty's loyal opposition fully understood the nature of his functions, he should say 'I take great pleasure in seconding this motion on behalf of the people whom we represent,' and this should be the end of the debate.

But since this Resolution is momentous in the history of the island, and since we have our ignoramuses, our criminals and our cut-throats – we do have our politically ambitious people of flexible views – it is necessary for me to make abundantly clear, and have recorded for all time, the reasons behind the government of this country bringing forward this resolution at this momentous stage.

Mr Speaker, you will be surprised to know that as recently as 1939, the leader of one of the parties on the other side, supported by a former Minister of Government, suggested to the Royal Commission after the disturbances in 1937 that Barbados should revert to a Crown Colony status when Jamaica had regained her original status. It is there in the records where Sir Grantley Adams suggested that, as a solution to the constitutional and economic problems of this country.

Today those of us on this side of the House have every cause, reason and justification to be angry at those people who would pull this island down for their own personal ambitions; we would have every reason to be angry at those people who do not even take time off to think who they are, where they have come from and where they are going.

When the Royal Commission came down here in 1939, exactly 300 years from the date when we began to run our own affairs, it was suggested seriously and supported by people who are in this House today and who are sitting on the opposite side of the Table, that Barbados should revert to Crown Colony status. The economic solution of the island's ills was that the island of Barbados should be developed into half-acre lots and a half-acre lot should be given to each family. That is again the Prime Minister of the late Federation. He did not elucidate on a point raised by Mr Morgan Jones as to whether his half an acre would be in Broad Street and my half an acre would be in Grave Yard, St Lucy,* but the artithmatic was interesting because, at the end of his proposal, Mr Morgan Jones asked Sir Grantley Adams what he was going to do with the other 60,000 people who would be left over. The reply was to 'Get rid of them,'. I am not trying to stir up any animosity against anyone. I am trying to illustrate that 300 years after the establishment of this ancient legislature, you still have people in Barbados who are incapable of thinking rightly, either for themselves or for the people whom they unfortunately represent.

Mr Speaker, despite my former association with that party, the people of Barbados forgave me as they forgave you and re-elected us in 1961 as the constitutional government of this country. We are now witnessing another unsuccessful attempt to take over the running of the country. We are still the constitutional government of this country, and, as such, the people have put us here to implement a certain programme, a programme which was put before the electorate in 1961.

You can compare the constitutional practice here in Barbados today with the practice in a neighbouring teritory, where without any recourse to the legislature, without any public debate whatsoever, without any warnings or discussion even with the closest confidants of the leader of the government himself, or people who considered themselves close to the government, it was announced that Trinidad and Tobago sought their independence. Up to today there has been no debate in Trinidad or Tobago about independence. There was a debate subsequent to the announcement of independence. Criticism of the draft constitution was sought from the Boys' Scouts and Girls' Guides, the Dorcas League, the Odd Fellows and such groups. That was the exercise in democracy that they went through. The exercise in democracy that we have gone through is that we stated our intention before an election. We faltered by the wayside to see if we could collect some of our lesser brethren – in the sense of more unfortunate brethren – together along the road to independence with us; that is where we wasted three and one half years in this exercise. Having been diverted from our main objective, we have merely returned to the mandate of the people and the expression of our

* Broad Street is the main street and commercial centre in the Barbados capital, Bridgetown; while the Parish of St Lucy is at the northern extreme of the island, and one of the most distant from Bridgetown.

intentions as demonstrated in the Manifesto of the Democratic Labour Party.

These are the facts. In 1961 on the 4th December when this government was returned, there was a Federation of the Westindies. That Federation was not dissolved until May 1962 by the Westindies Federation Dissolution Act of April of that year, and the Westindies Dissolution Act made provision by order in Council to take away, to confer and otherwise to deal with the constitutions of all territories in this area; and it is rather ironic, Mr Speaker, that the Federation should have broken up on the very day on which, by the recommendation of the 1961 Conference in London, it was supposed to have become independent. The two richest territories seceded with the consent and approval, and I will go so far as to say, with the connivance of Her Majesty's Government. Shortly thereafter we journeyed to London, and the result of our labours was a Command Paper laid before Parliament, and also laid in this legislature, No. 1746, which sets out certain proposals for a Federation.

Mr Speaker, I just want to say that when you hear the talk mooted about in the atmosphere about independence in a Federation, I want to know what Federation they are talking about. It could not be an existing Federation, because there is no Westindies Federation existing today, and there has not been a Federation of the Westindies since 1962...a Federation does not exist in fact or in law between us and the other seven territories in the Eastern Caribbean.

It was clear from 1963 to all of us who were engaged almost in mortal combat with Her Majesty's Secretary of State and his legal advisers that the British government had no confidence in any Federation of the Eastern Caribbean, and no intention to make any capital or other contribution to a Federation. The British government is now prepared to make contributions to individual territories, provided they can keep their eyes on their money; and when you consider the context in which the Constitution of Grenada was taken away, and what was happening in other Windward and Leeward Island territories in financial mismanagement, you cannot blame the British government for keeping a careful eye on the taxpayers' money.

I remember I woke up one morning earlier this year in a cold sweat; I do not know what was agitating my mind, and at the first light of dawn, I telephoned the Honourable Minister of Education (J. Cameron Tudor, now the Foreign Minister, Sir James Tudor) and told him my experience a couple of hours before and I said these four words: 'They nearly had us'. It was because I had been working over the draft Federal Scheme in preparation for a document which was subsequently published and laid in this House. We were going into this exercise in all good faith with our eyes shut, because like in so many other departments of life, we assumed that what we are accustomed to, prevails in other places and will continue to be so for ever more hereafter.

We assumed that we were going into a federation and that there would be the same degree of financial integrity, the same respect for constitutional propriety as exists in this island. Mr Speaker, I just want to say that I am a Westindian, and there is no one who is more Westindian either by birth or by inclination or otherwise than I am. I always refrain from disclosing any legislative matters which I know about, which would be detrimental to the successful carrying out of the federal exercise. I did nothing that an atmosphere of recrimination should be introduced at any stage, and so I suppressed matters which should have better seen the light of day. I do not think by doing so I betrayed the trust of honourable members of the House, because my motives were altruistic.

If I make a statement of fact about our statistics on crime, this is not anything to be anoyed about. If I say that Dr. Williams[**] said that the proposal to have freedom of movement would create serious problems which Trinidad could not support and did not intend to support even after the end of ten years, is this supposed to be abuse of your neighbours? These are unfortunate factors of colonialism. There are some people in Barbados who would want to tell you that there is no such thing as colonialism and that we are British subjects and that we are happy to be called British subjects. But the worst thing about colonialism is this:- These islands in the Eastern Caribbean only began to get off the ground since they were taken over by democratic goverments in their islands which were responsible to the people. No one is going to be content to be treated as second class citizens in perpetuity. No one is going to be content to sit down indefinitely and watch places like Gambia, Togoland, Malta with only 95 square miles and even the Cook Islands that no school child has heard about, islands with a total population of 11,000 and 12,000 and with populations smaller than many constituencies of ours, being represented and sitting around the United Nations table.

Nobody in this party wants a seat in the United Nations for prestige purposes. Our stand is for the people of Barbados in perpetuity; it is the only state which the Almighty God has ordained.

[**] Dr. Eric Williams, the late Prime Minister of Trinidad and Tobago.

71

I should like to make the position of my government abundantly clear. When we decided unilaterally – and I say unilaterally because without any reference to the people of Barbados, I took independent members of the House, the Leader of the Opposition and others to conferences to see if we could patch together the wreckage of the former Federation; I think that we were overly ambitious, but no one can blame us for trying. What I find strange is that having confessed that we are not the creators of mankind and that we could not succeed in doing what the Almighty did not do when he brought certain people into this world, that is to put sense in their heads, I do not think that this government should be vilified for taking the people of Barbados on the road to independence that we had digressed from in 1962 and thereafter. To me this is the strangest situation that could exist in any country with ancient traditions like this one.

You would not expect, Sir, after discussing this matter for three and a half years, how surprised we were to hear all of a sudden that members on the other side were championing the pursuit of the Federal dream. For three and a half years, Chief Ministers of the other colonies were coming up here discussing, not only problems relating to the Federation, but we were giving them advice and encouraging their people to come to Barbados to work to the detriment of the people of this country. In the meantime, not one of them on the opposite side had the decency to ask a Chief Minister to come to his home and have a cup of tea. There are some members over there who would not even ask some members of the House to come to their homes and have a cup of tea. We are living in a country in which you can be sitting next to a boy in Harrison College*** and in the evening after school, he passes you by as if you never existed. That is the kind of people which you find in these islands. We in Barbados, more than any other people in any part of the world, have exhibited how not to live together in unity, and there are no greater practitioners of this than the honourable members on the other side who now claim to be the champions of the people from the other islands.

We would never get together in the Westindies until we fashion something of our own. We have a peculiar situation in the Westindies. There is no political formula that you can translate from Europe or America, that can have application to a situation such as what we have inherited here in the Westindies.

Mr Speaker, I shall continue to read from the Resolution which we have before us: 'any movement towards integration of the people of

*** A prestigious secondary school in Bridgetown.

the area must spring not only from a natural desire for independence, but primarily from a reasonable expectation, if not a certainty of economic advantage. The movement must be sustained by a full appreciation and understanding of its implications and by mutual respect and sincereity of purpose.'

That is what we are being criticised for today. We have said that none of these experiments has been a success. People like the late Professor Ivor Jennings, when they wrote on the Federal Constitution, although realising the difficulties and stating certain prerequisites of Federation, they were not able sufficiently to break down their analysis to be an accurate guide to people who were embarking on this exercise for the first time. Only a Westindian who is working with Westindians, or a Malaysian who is working with Malaysians today will understand the full implications of the Federal exercise. It is one of the most difficult of exercises.

The Federation broke up when two colonies seceded and three others pulled out. I told Sir Stephen Luke that we were not here to work as scavengers; we do not want to have a Federation at all costs with the loss of our self-respect. We were very careful during our campaign not to create any atmosphere of embarrassment for the government that was in power then by campaigning against their breaking up of the Federation.

I do not want anybody to get up and ask any stupid questions in this House. Nobody is going to advise us. There is no provision in this island for a referendum, and as long as this government is in power, there is not going to be one. As long as this government is in power, there is not going to be any proportional representation. We have had a direct franchise all this time. The only electoral reform we promised to do is to abolish the anachronism of dual-member constituencies. As far as electoral reform is concerned, there is no electoral reform to be performed in this island; we have fought and won those battles.

I am merely stating the constitutional position of the government vis-à-vis the electorate of this island. I am not making any proclamation of dictatorship.

I am a penniless politician, but I want to remain an honest one; and if you want to be honest to the people, you have to tell them the plain facts of life. If they do not like the decisions taken by the Government in office, they have recourse to the ballot box. This is what we call a democratic system of government, and as long as this government is in office, we will stick to that.

People must understand that a good government is put there to make decisions. I have to make decisions on the part of the people of this island. You can sleep better in your bed because we make these decisions. As a matter of fact, a democratic government functions best with organised opinion. It virtually amounts to this, that at election time the people place the decision and policy power into your hands. To make you keep on a straight and narrow path, the political party should normally declare its intention in what is called a manifesto.

Therefore, you have two checks. You have the ballot box and you have to publish a programme in what is called a manifesto; otherwise any man can get up on a public platform and say whatever he likes.

If you have a declaration of your intention towards the people of this island, then the people of this island can check your declaration against your performances, and that is the test, and the only test, which will be applied to a government in a democracy. The test is not to buy votes by bribes; and you can never in a democracy hope to get rid of the government in that way. You can only remove the government when the people are dissatisfied with that government. The government has been put there to make decisions and this government has made a decision. I want it to go down on the record of this House because I am an angry man.

Mr Speaker, when you are in a country you owe loyalty first to that country. You can have difficulties and differences, whether the country is an independent country or whether the country is a non self-governing territory or whether it is a grant-aided territory, the society – meaning the government, because that is the policy-making sector of the society – has to draw the line between allowable conduct on the one hand, and insanity or crime on the other.

Some people are talking as if today is the beginning of creation. We have a country and we have a constitution. We have laws, we have police forces, and we are not going to invent police forces any more than we are going to invent crimes or criminals or sadists. We have them in society. If anybody goes to gaol, it is because he has been going to gaol for a long time and because we have been vigilant enough to send him to gaol; but we have a country and this is the meaning of having a country.

People of this country try to set white people against black people. Some members over there would rally members of European descent in this population and tell them that Barrow intends to do so-and-so. They do not have enough sense to ask what is his intention. Never has anybody in this political party expressed or implied any intention that this government or this country should proceed along anything different from an orderly path to independence. The constitution which we are operating now is the type of constitution which we will be operating after independence.

They talk about independence within a Federation; this is the kind of independence which did not dawn on me until I woke up in a nightmare at 3 o'clock in the morning and found myself covered in perspiration, because several activities which were going on in the periphery were beginning to bother me in the back of my mind, and I was watching the behaviour of certain people, and I tried to analyse why it was that certain people were so dead set on certain things. I looked at the Federal Constitution until about 1 o'clock that morning in my office, went home, made a cup of tea and went to bed and woke up in cold sweats. Mr (Vere) Bird (then Chief Minister now Prime Minister of Antigua) has all the seats because the people gave him all. 'The Lord giveth and the Lord taketh away: Blessed be the name of the Lord.' Some of them over there will get their seats taken away; so be it. No one has a claim to political immortality; there are no political immortals under our constitution. You cannot give yourself immortality. As a matter of fact, I would like to say that anybody who made himself President of a country for his life time was automatically signing his death warrant, because that is the only way you could remove him. Only an inept person would make himself President for life. If a man makes himself President for life, you cannot get rid of him the constitutional way, but you can get rid of him by assassination.

We talk of psychological injuries that have been done to our young people by instilling in them a sense of inferiority. There are people in this House who have said they would never employ a black man before they employ a white man. People who are editors in this country would not invite a black man to their house unless they want to sell some idea to him. Therefore, let us understand the various heads of survival. You have survival of being able to fight against the invading hordes of Nazi Germany or any aggressor. You have survival of the human personality. You have economic survival. These are very important factors in human existence. These are very important survivals.

They are not in need of emancipation: they are prisoners in chains. They are the people who respond only to the stimulus of money and they do not care what the stimulus of money will do. There is no political party outside of our party in Barbados which has a clearly defined ideology and perspective for the people of this island, and that is why they are against it.

If you can get independence and economic advantage without having a constitutional superstructure imposed upon you, there is absolutely no inducement and no valid reason why a country like Barbados should surrender to the Lesser Antilles, that is, the less politically astute and experienced politicians of the Lesser Antilles, and I make no apology for saying it. If I say that I do not consider that this government should engage in these federal discussions until after independence, I am merely guaranteeing the independence of the people of Barbados if we go into a federation first. It is as simple as that.

I want to say this: it is one thing to be critical of politicians in the small areas and about the way they function; but these are systems which were set up by Her Majesty's Government when they used to run their affairs and nobody know what they did. These ministers have inherited problems and worries, and the islands were in a condition where all the services and institutions were dilapidated and run-down. These are countries which have been exploited until the last drop of blood has been squeezed out of them, and, under these circumstances, you cannot be surprised if the British government wants to palm off these islands and wants others to take them on.

I have the profoundest respect for the country where I had part of my education, and for the good things in it; but the point is that this is the parting of the ways, and when you come to the parting of the ways, you should be able to continue in correspondence without any acrimony.

I am not going to go into a long recital of all that has not been done in these territories, which is the reason for the present impasse. Colonialism is the reason for the present impasse in Westindian affairs, and we cannot afford to wait. I am not going into a recital of what the British have done and what they have not done. Their relation with our people has not been a happy association. It has been a very unhappy association, and it is regrettable that we will have some of the downtrodden, who feel that they are now slightly privileged, fighting on the side of the people who perpetrated all these acts of inhumanity against our people. When I go to a conference and I want to tell the Secretary of State to go to hell or to know his place, I tell him so because I know the premises, and the position of strength from which I am speaking is not a position of feeling inferior in any way. They are the people who should feel inferior, because they are the people who have broken every single law of morality as far as a relationship with us is concerned. This is all the more reason why we should stand on our own feet, because people are not going to respect you, Sir, if despite the fact that you are financially independent, you still want to be deemed to be a second class citizen of another country.

This is a moment in our history of which we should all be proud instead of being ashamed. If I have any sense of shame, it is shame to know that in my country there still exists an element, that, despite all we have gone through we still have people who are so degrading, and people who are so tantalised by the trappings of colonialism. I do not want my children to grow up as second class citizens, and I do not want the children of any of the ladies who work for me in my house assisting us in the discharge of our daily duties, or the man who works in the garden, or the man who drives the proverbial omnibus to grow up with any sense of inferiority to any persons.

Independence does not mean that you become disrespectful to anyone provided he respects you; and I know that Barbadians have enough good sense; they have a reputation for being polite and courteous to people, and the fact that we have independence would not mean that we are animals cut loose and starting to run around in circles, because we have been operating an independent constitution all these years.

I do not want to embarrass the Secretary of State or any other government. I make the decision about elections and this is a constitutional right. This is not a right which I have arrogated unto myself in my search for dictatorial power or any nonsense like that. How dishonest can people get in this country? When you examine it, you will find that the people who go in for this kind of vilification have not got a single achievement to their credit, a single achievement which has been the subject of impartial examination by anybody inside a school or university or outside; not a single political achievement for the years they are supposed, like the last government, to have spent in here. The only achievement they have is the achievement of slander and degradation; but they underestimate the intelligence of the masses of this country, because the masses of this country want independence. The masses of this country have too much sense to aspire to get into company which is intellectually inferior to the African heritage; but we have a bunch of humbugs in this country whose only ambition is to identify themselves with the hegemony, the presiding power, of Great Britain, people who look like British people and, therefore, are associated with the presiding power, and, if they get into their company, they feel that some of this prestige will rub off on them. That is why they do not want independence, because when you remove the tutelage of subservience and the bonds which keep you down, then every man is the same man. This is a psychological problem.

Mr Deputy Speaker, it depresses me particularly and the members of my Party, because we recognise analytically that this is one of the sad effects of colonialism. I really would be disappointed in a certain way because I thought that with the long tradition we have in Barbados, when we have had to stare facts in the face, and knowing that the people think about us, we would see that they are economically and culturally opposed to the masses of this country. The masses of a country are the true people in every country and they know it, and to try to fool the masses is to underestimate the intelligence of the masses.

What I find rather depressing in the whole exercise, is that they know we have a Constitution, because they have been living under a Constitution and working under the Constitution insofar as it suited them. When it did not suit them, they committed breaches of the constitutional proprieties. If I say, therefore, that I cannot view their activities with any sense of respect as a Barbadian, it is because I am a Barbadian and I am a loyal Barbadian. Anybody who knows me would know well enough that I have no ambition. This is one of my stumbling blocks all my life. I probably would have been a lot further if I had ambition. I have certain principles; they may be Victorian and you may consider them ingenuous. Because of the modern-day thought of 'dog eat dog', some people think that anybody who thinks in Victorian terms is out of date and not 'with it'. Therefore, among some people it is an expedient thing to accept money for political favours dispensed as part and parcel of what they call the game of politics. But it is not a game with us; it is a serious business. I see issues directly in terms of black and white, and there are no gradations between them as far as I am concerned; but there are people in this country and other countries, too, who consider politics a game. They make the pretext that they would do this and that for the people and that kind of thing. They do not want the people to get too much, because if you do all the things for the people that should be done for them, the State would then wither away and you would no longer continue to be an important personage.

If you give a man the right to work for his own living at a wage he considers compatible with his aspirations for himself and his children, then you do not have any more hold over him; but if you can keep him in a state of degradation and make him feel inferior, then they will always use you as the buffer between his oppressors and himself, and this is the role assumed by too many politicians in

Barbados for too long. This is the role which has been assumed by too many of our politicians in Barbados, content to be the buffer element between the masses and the people who do not participate in the society. They only bleed certain people; they do not communicate with them except during business hours. This is the kind of society we are against and they know we are against it. It is not a question of black or white, because we have more black political humbugs than we have white humbugs, and we have them right here in the House (of Assembly), unfortunately. There are certain things, for instance, that some members on the other side would stoop to which the honourable junior member for Christ Church (a white businessman, Fred Goddard) would never stoop to; he does not have to, and he knows he would incur, probably, the animosity of his party if he did them; but other people do these things which are detrimental to the society and they get applauded for it, because to be smart in this society you have to scramble over somebody. It does not matter how you get there; all will be forgiven. It does not matter how many people you assassinate or how many people you put to death or how many people are deprived of their livelihood; it does not matter as long as you get there; when you get there like Morgan the pirate, and all the other rogues and villains of history like Lord Nelson, you will be crowned with imperial honours at the end.

If we go back then in making this analysis of Westindian society, we have been made this way by our history. It has been a history of oppression, and some of us are in a hurry to dissociate ourselves from this long history of oppression, and they are so stupid, they have become so imbued with the spirit of cynicism that they are unaware that the quickest way to get away from this long history of oppression is for all the people to get away, and not a few of them climbing to the top of the ladder and kicking it down behind them.

All of us have to escape; there are not a few of us escaping. What does it profit a man to be Prime Minister of Barbados or of the Westindies? What does it mean? It means nothing if you lose your soul and achieve these objectives. What can you do for a man who is living at subsistence level after you have profited and have acquired all of these material comforts? How many meals a day can you eat? I want to tell some of the young professional people in this country that nobody has ever been revered in history for having become the richest man.

People do not respect you for getting into a certain position. Nobody respects me or would respect the ministers of government or any Premier of Barbados if they go in for corruption. With all the slander and lies which members of the opposition have told on me, if any of them can stand up and say that anybody paid me five dollars, I will hold my peace. I will hold my peace if anybody would get up and say that I have accepted money for doing anything corrupt. A lot of them over there cannot say that. I have never been fortunate enough to win a sweepstake, but I do not intend to get my hands soiled for them or anybody else. I have to discharge my duty to the programme which has been laid down by us and to the people of Barbados and those are the premises from which I am speaking. Some of them are so corrupt that they cannot understand how none of us on this side of the House are not. Corruption is something to them which is crowned with precious stones in these days, when you look around and see 'bauball' going around – to use a good Trinidadian expression. Some people feel that you must try and get as rich as possible in the shortest possible time.

This political conduct appears to be notable today. However, when you have finished, look at Batista of Cuba[****] and all other people like him! Mussolini of Italy was hanged upside down. He was the leader of one of the largest countries in Europe. Look at how Hitler ended up. Where are all of them today? But the names of the liberators, however poor they were, would remain. Simon Bolivar died a poor man on a little island called Margarita off the north coast of Venezuela. Look at liberators like Alexander Hamilton, George Washington, Touissant L'Ouverture. They were in a position where they could have been corrupted, but they did not allow themselves to be corrupted. When the history of Barbados in 1966 is written all the people who have participated in this exercise of trying to pull down what we have built up for Barbados, posterity would have their names desecrated in every sense of the term, and if posterity could dig up their bones or hang them in effigy, posterity would do that – do not let any of them have any illusions. This is a very serious matter. After the country had been exposed during the last three months – three months which we allowed for democratic discussion – to the sort of sordid conduct that has been witnessed and to our having mercenaries like the white bastards in the Belgian Congo – and it is a historical fact that even in the African countries, they employed white mercenaries to shoot down their own people – that even in this country of Barbados you find the white people hiring black people to keep back their own people. I want to tell you this. I rejoice because the Almighty moves in a mysterious way, his

[****]Fulencia Batista, Cuban dictator ousted in a populist rebellion led by Fidel Castro in 1959.

wonders to perform, because what this exercise has done more than anything else, is to separate the sheep from the goats, the honest from the dishonest and the liars from the leaders.

What it has done is to separate the sheep from the goats. It has purged the conscience of the community of the disharmonious elements. This has acted as a catalyst to bring up to the surface everything that is wrong in a community like this. We have learnt one lesson, and one lesson alone, that is how not to live together in unity.

We have evolved a formula for living together, but not having any strength. This is one of the paradoxes of our colonial situation in Barbados. Things are improving, but they are not what they should be and there are many things which we have experienced since this Resolution was laid in this House. The White Paper was laid before the legislature in August, and the Resolution was tabled afterwards. We have allowed three months for free unbridled discussion in this country. I know of no other country, including the United States and the United Kingdom, where the people who exhibit these disruptive propensities would be allowed to walk about the capital with impunity. I say that without any reservation. That in itself shows that we have had to purge ourselves of the things which have existed in the community for all of these years. The masses have begun to speak for themselves, and long may they continue to do so.

The soul of this community has to be laid bare, and there is no better time to do that than when we are preparing for independence, so that we know what we are, who we are, and where we are going.

The people who have money in this country are uncultured and they have no use for nine-tenths of the people of this country. Look at their houses. All they want to know is how much profit they are going to make and how much money they are going to lose. They do not understand the first thing of the complexities of the system.

Who are all these people and what have they contributed to the society? Nothing. They do not like the legislation we pass, and I am not asking them to like it. They are not going to like the Tenantries Bill and they are not going to like the Social Securities Bill. They do not like these things because they feel people are becoming too independent. They have no cultural standing; they have no political ideology; they are only in an entrenched position of privilege and prestige, of prestige inherited by the association with the metropolitan country which is always willing to run to their rescue.

I want to say something about the metropolitan country. Right here in my White Paper I have referred to the Central African Federation which lasted from 1953 to 1963. The Central African Federation was dissolved in 1963 because of Dr. Kenneth Kaunda and Dr. Hastings Banda, the respective leaders of their people. Both of them have been in gaol for agitating for freedom for their people; so what did the British government do? They threw them into a Federation with Southern Rhodesia in 1953, and put Dr. Kaunda and Dr. Banda in gaol, and the effect of this Federation was to give 200,000 white Rhodesians perpetual dominance over four million Africans in South Rhodesia, and God knows how many in what used to be Nyasaland and Northern Rhodesia and which are now Malawi and Zambia respectively.

Sir Grantley Adams' Federation was a dependent Federation, a Crown Colony Federation, and in desperation Mr (Norman) Manley (then Premier of Jamaica) and Dr. (Eric) Williams (then Premier of Trinidad and Tobago) called a conference in England which was to make the Federation independent on the 31st of May, 1962. That was the date set for the independence of the Westindies Federation, but it was broken up on the same date. The British government broke it up on that date.

I have come across in the United Kingdom some of the crudest people I have ever come across in my life and some of us try to ape all the worst features of the English educational system.

When you talk about political immorality, you have to understand that there is a country which has ruthlessly taken hold of the economy of the other countries, people who are more benighted than ourselves and less advanced in what they choose to call a civilisation; they have murdered, detribalised and suppressed their religious activities and that sort of thing, forbidding them to use their own language. You cannot be surprised that the residual effects of that kind of harsh treatment must still be manifested in the behaviour of some politicians of the colonial territories today.

What I want to impress upon honourable members is that there is nothing politically moral in the exercise of this Federation at all. In other words, it was the device to get rid of the incorrigible politicians of the Leeward and Windward Islands who were causing them (the British government) quite a lot of headaches. At the same time, there will be people of a certain mealy-mouthed, holier-than-thou attitude who would say that they have created another territory free to a state of independence, as if the whole experience was some sort of Sunday School exercise, and not one of the worst things which could be perpetrated in the history of mankind.

Errol Walton Barrow's finest, and proudest hour!!

Independence Day 1966. Months of sometimes bitter and acrimonious debate behind him, Prime-Minister designate, Errol Walton Barrow (at right), offers the victory sign to thousands of Barbadians who packed a small race track just south of Bridgetown to participate in the flag-raising ceremony.

The Union Jack is hauled down for the last time, and Barbados' own Broken Trident is hoisted in its place, signalling the end of three centuries of British rule.

Mr Barrow's hand is triumphantly held aloft by the island's first Governor-General, Sir John Stow.

Boating was one of Errol Walton Barrow's favourite past-times. In these photographs, he is seen in the above (second from right), being briefed on the controls of one vessel, and in the other (page 85), relaxing in the company of his friend, James Mitchell, now Prime Minister of St. Vincent and the Grenadines.

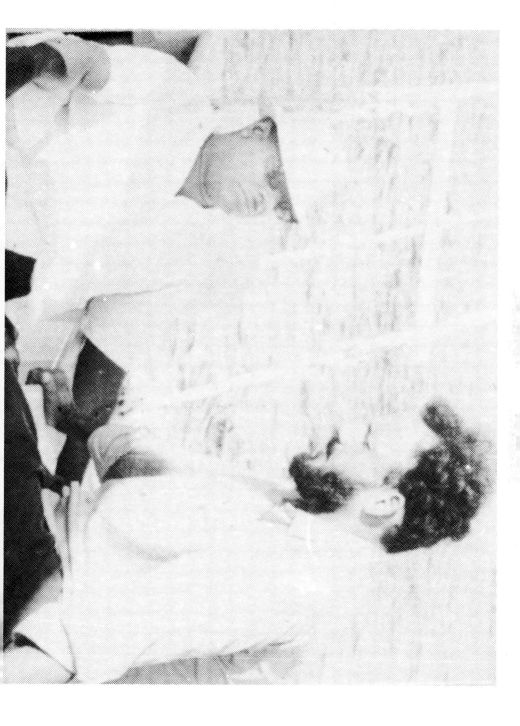

Then Premier Errol Walton Barrow in a quiet moment, eyes shut, hands in pockets, in his own thoughts.
This photograph was taken in Canada in November 1965.

86

"No loitering on colonial premises"

Address to the Barbados Constitutional Conference in London, July 1966

Mr Secretary of State,

We thank you for the courtesies which you have so far shown us and particularly for the kind words of welcome you have just spoken.

The small territory whose fortune and future we are met here to decide, is unique in many respects. It came into association with the Crown of England neither by conquest nor by purchase but by settlement. It is interesting to note that Barbados began its association with England at the time when English political institutions experienced their severest strain.

When in 1639 your own country had been governed without a Parliament for 11 years, the English inhabitants of Barbados settled a Parliament for themselves and thereby created the Legislative institutions which we have since, without any disturbance enjoyed. In this respect, Barbados shared only with Virginia, Massachusetts and Bermuda, the solid comforts of representative government.

In 1651, when Englishmen were cowering in their homes under the whip of Cromwell's major-generals, and when they who had lopped off the head of a king sought to enmesh the people of Barbados in their 'saintly' tyranny, Barbadians stubbornly defended their respective institutions from Cromwell and in the famous Charter of Barbados which they signed, they have managed to preserve for three centuries the supremacy of parliaments and the liberty of the subject.

A century and a half later, the genius of Thomas Jefferson distilled from this Charter that heady wine of sovereignty which we now know as the Declaration of American Independence.

Again when in 1668 the crown and the liberties of England were once more in jeopardy, and the democratic freedoms had to be enshrined in a Bill of Rights, the Parliament of Barbados celebrated its golden jubilee and judges administered the same common and statute law which was under a temporary cloud in England.

The strength and durability of our institutions are best demonstrated by the fact that representative government and the rule of law are now administered by people who are different in racial origins from those who established them.

Ninety per cent of our people are of African origin, whose ancestors have experienced the harshness of unfree and unrequited labour. Their descendants have lived through the period since emancipation hemmed in by all the frustrations which a plantation economy imposes upon its labour force.

As opportunities came, they fought and finally broke the political power of the local oligarchy, and now enjoy full internal self-government, based on adult suffrage at the age of 18, a Cabinet system, an independent judiciary, a competent public service, a population which is 98 per cent literate – most significant of all a Treasury which has never needed a grant in aid of administration.

The people who now enjoy these blessings feel a natural affinity with, and are grateful to, those Englishmen who in 1639 built better than they knew. They laid the foundations for that free society, a small part of which we already experience and the greater portion of which we shall establish after independence.

Our relations with the Crown have always been warm and it is the unanimous desire of our citizens that Her Majesty shall be Queen and Head of State of an independent Barbados.

Occasionally in our history, we had to resist the encroachments of British governments in our internal affairs, encroachments designed to lower the status from that of a settled territory to that of a colony.

In 1876, the Legislature of Barbados successfully defeated an attempt by the Colonial Office to force our country into a federation which, if it had come about, would have given the Colonial Office greater control over Barbadian affairs.

In defeating that manoeuvre, we embarked on the path along which our Constitution has been carried to the threshold of Independence.

When, therefore, the Legislature of Barbados in January, in affirmative and convincing manner, requested your predecessor to arrange this conference, the Legislature itself was playing its traditional role of speaking for the people in their great moments.

In our country, as in England, the supremacy of Parliament is zealously upheld and a Government of Barbados, like its counterpart in Britain, would never resort to any subterfuge designed to frustrate the clearly expressed desires of a duly elected Parliament.

In order that you, Mr Secretary of State, should not be incommoded by our problems,we have assumed and discharged the responsibility for producing the constitution under which the people of Barbados will continue to govern themselves after independence.

As you expect in a country with our parliamentary traditions, this constitution was presented in draft, first to our Legislature and then to our citizens. Only as recently as Friday last, it was given final approval in its amended form, and the draft is now submitted for your consideration.

In our view, there can be no question whether Barbados is ripe and ready for independence. Three centuries of history answer that question in the affirmative. You have never had to shore up our finances; you have never had to maintain or preserve public order among us. Even now, without the help of thousands of our best citizens, your own hospital and transport system would be in jeopardy.

In two world wars, hundreds of our people have readily responded to your summons and some have never returned. The People of Barbados have never given you any cause for worry, and no British government has ever been forced, on our account to vindicate its policy at the bar of international opinion.

In assuming the burdens of independence, the people of Barbados have no illusions about their task. They are well aware that in this country, it is commonly believed, although it is not a fact, that people of African origin cannot for long maintain democratic forms of government after independence.

These people conveniently forget that the colonial system was designed not to promote free institutions, but to safeguard imperial interests. They also forget that if in the act of surrendering power, the imperial authority promotes and leaves behind it, a divided community, then some time must necessarily elapse before democratic institutions can take root in countries emerging from colonialism.

Political democracy is a precious concept, but it is not an Anglo-Saxon discovery and it is capable of growth among all sorts and conditions of people. Even in Anglo-Saxon countries, the principles of democracy are not always adhered to when justice is required for persons of different racial origins.

In the face of this, it is not surprising that new countries must take time to develop free institutions. To expect an emergent country to provide a fully democratic system on the morning after a colonial nightmare, is rather like asking a man to explore England with a map of Old Sarum and an 18th Century map at that.

By some fortunate turn of history, the people of Barbados have managed to establish before their independence the solid framework of a free society. Their training and apprenticeship are now complete. They have three centuries of steady maturity to draw on and self-confidence sprung from the management of their own affairs.

Neither the smallness of their territory nor the slenderness of their physical resources deters them in the path to nationhood. They have a modest part to play in the affairs of their region, the Common-wealth and the world, and all they require from you, is that you should speed them to their rendezvous with destiny sometime in 1966.

Mr Secretary, we have a self-imposed curfew on the duration of these discussions in that the government has arranged to leave the United Kingdom on the 5th of July for an equally important meeting with our partners in Canada.

There can be no time in the circumstances for the lowing herd to wind slowly o'er the Lee.

This, Sir, is in accord with your wishes and our intention to safeguard your person even if your office is soon to be dissolved. My Government, I assure you, Sir, will not be found loitering on colonial premises after closing time.

Friends of all; satellites of none

Address to the United Nations, on the occasion of the admission of Barbados to membership of the UN, December 1966.

Mr President,
Mr Secretary General,
Distinguished Delegates,

Humility must be the most appropriate feeling for the leader of a state admitted to membership of this illustrious assembly on the basis of sovereign equality.

The people of Barbados, even before their emergence into nationhood, have always tried, not without some success, to arrange their affairs in accordance with the principles of this Charter to which I have, in their name, subscribed their unstinted allegiance. Despite the limitation of their territory, the paucity of their numbers, the slenderness of their resources, the inhibiting atmosphere of three centuries of colonialism, they have provided for themselves stable political institutions and economic activities which will better stimulate their future development.

In their name, we wish to thank the governments of the Argentine, Britain, New Zealand, Nigeria and Uganda for their prompt and generous sponsorship of our country. We also thank the distinguished delegates here assembled for the warm and courteous greeting accorded to our delegation. We should like to record our profound appreciation to all the distinguished members of the Security Council for the alacrity with which they processed our application to make it possible for us to secure membership in the same year that we achieved nationhood.

The people of Barbados do not draw a dividing line between their internal affairs and their foreign policy. They strive in their domestic arrangements to create a just society for themselves. In their Constitution, they affirm respect for the Rule of Law; they also declare their intention to establish and maintain the kind of society which enables each citizen, to the full extent of his capacity, to play his part in the national life; they further resolve that their economic system, as it develops, must be equitably administered and enjoyed and that undeviating recognition should be paid to ability, integrity and merit.

In thus charting our domestic course, we can have no interest in a foreign policy which contradicts our national goals. On the contrary, we will support genuine efforts at world peace because our society is stable. We will strenuously assist the uprooting of vestigial imperialisms because our institutions are free. We will press for the rapid economic growth of all underdeveloped countries because we are busily engaged in building up our own. *In fine*, our foreign and domestic policies are the obverse and reverse sides of a single coin.

We have devised the kind of foreign policy which is consistent with our national situation and which is also based on the current realities of international politics.

We have no quarrels to pursue and we particularly insist that we do not regard any member states as our natural opponent. We shall not involve ourselves in sterile ideological wranglings because we are exponents not of the diplomacy of power, but of the diplomacy of peace and prosperity. We will not regard any great power as necessarily right in a given dispute unless we are convinced of this, yet at the same time we will not view the great powers with perennial suspicion merely on account of their size, their wealth, or their nuclear potential. We will be friends of all, satellites of none.

A disquieting feature of the world situation is the frequent allusion made to the alleged proliferation of small states in this Assembly. Attempts are made from time to time to devise schemes to give the larger countries more voting power in the Assembly. The principle of 'one state one vote' whereby all member states are equal under the Charter, is becoming unfashionable and the proponents of the new theory wish to render some states more equal than others.

The General Assembly should know that the Barbados Delegation will not support any formula based on such a preposterous bit of special pleading. To accept it even for the narrow purposes of discussion at any time, would be to connive at the negation of democratic principle. The whole basis on which this organisation rests, is that of equal sovereignty. If size, wealth or capacity to destroy mankind were the basis for membership, the organisation would not exist in its present form and its Security Council would consist of a mere handful of mutually suspicious countries.

It seems strange to small countries to find their equality challenged by these mutterings of discontent with the form of the Charter. Perhaps the mightier nations genuinely fear that their influence will be swamped in the majority of votes now recorded in this Assembly. This fear can only be real if the mighty are pursuing aims inimical to the interests of the smaller ones. So long as their own national interests and their international commitments can be identified with those of the small countries, they have no reason to fear the admission of small states to this Assembly. Democratic countries owe the stability of their institutions to the participation of the masses in the political life of their countries. In like manner, the emergence of small states into full sovereignty increases the chances of peace.

Even in this distinguished Assembly, it is not always, or not fully, appreciated that the tensions of the cold war have been lessened by the mere existence of nearly forty newly independent states in Africa, Asia and the Caribbean. United Nations opinion is now more often to be found in Delhi, Addis Ababa and Port-of-Spain than it is in London, Moscow and Washington. No longer is there that unique and frightening confrontation of rival power blocs staring and scuffling with each other in the ruins of their respective policies. The independent countries of Africa, Asia, the Caribbean and the other uncommitted countries are making, by their existence alone, an outstanding contribution to international stability.

If the larger countries wish to earn or to retain the confidence and respect of small countries, there will have to be a rapid change of values. They must no longer enjoy squatters' rights in the volume and arrangement of world trade. New concepts of distribution and exchange will have to be worked out, because emergent countries will no longer be content to be hewers of wood and drawers of water while the wealth of the world flows past them into the coffers of some twenty countries.

In a world population of some 2,400,000,000, only 375,000,000 (or slightly less than one-sixth) enjoy the best standards of living. In another segment of the world population, some 425,000,000 (or slightly more than one-sixth) enjoy fairly tolerable standards of living. The remainder of mankind, some 1,600,000,000 souls in Asia, Africa, South Eastern Europe, Latin America and the Caribbean, sweat out their lives in unremitting poverty, without the tools of modern production, with meagre educational facilities, with little expertise in the arts of public administration, with driblets of financial and technical assistance, with a population explosion and with a cataract of gratuitous advice on how to govern themselves.

The stark reality of the international situation is not the possibility of nuclear destruction, but the certainty of dissolution if this mass misery continues beyond this current decade. When 65 per cent of the world's population can enjoy only 19 per cent of the world's wealth, a diplomacy based on power cannot withstand the explosive anger of upheaval based on poverty. Two-thirds of the world's people do not fear a nuclear holocaust because they literally have nothing to live for. The irony of their situation is that they hold the key to the world's prosperity, but that the doors are bolted against them by the participants of prosperity.

This is the background, distinguished delegates, against which my small country enters upon its international obligations. It belongs to the submerged two-thirds of the world. It sees no hope for itself or for its companions in misery except in the efforts made in this Assembly to work out with speed, the new conditions of human progress. The Barbados delegation pays its tribute to the specialised agencies of this body for the solid contribution made both in the past and now, to human well-being in many parts of the globe. But this delegation nevertheless feels that the eradication of world poverty is a function which cannot be discharged by delegation, but must engage the United Nations at their highest levels.

The obligation laid on the Security Council to preserve world peace ought to be amplified by an equally solemn commitment to prevent world poverty. It is not a coincidence that the explosive areas of the world are precisely those areas in which ignorance and poverty most abound.

Mr President,

Mr Secretary-General

Distinguished Delegates,

The people of Barbados will support and uphold the efforts of this organisation to the limit of their moral and physical resources and would wish to record their profound gratitude to the Assembly for this first great privilege of expressing their hopes and aspirations for the unity and progress of mankind. They could best sum up their attitude to this moment of their history in the words of Mr 'Valiant for Truth', an interesting character in John Bunyan's famous book:

'Though with much difficulty I have got hither,
'Yet I do not repent me of the trouble I have taken.'

"Towards a United Caribbean"

Statement made in the House of Assembly on June 19, 1973, on the establishment of the Caribbean Community

At the conclusion of the Eighth Conference of Heads of Government of Commonwealth Caribbean Countries, held in Georgetown, Guyana, in April this year, the Minister of External Affairs signed on behalf of the Government of Barbados, the Georgetown Accord which was adopted at that conference.

Under that instrument, the governments of Barbados, Guyana, Jamaica and Trinidad and Tobago undertook to sign and ratify a Community Treaty in order to establish a Caribbean Community and Common Market as between their respective countries with effect from August 1, 1973.

The governments of Belize, Dominica, Grenada, St Kitts-Nevis-Anguilla, St Lucia, St Vincent, undertook to sign and ratify the Treaty so as to become parties thereto on 1st May, 1974, whereas the governments of Antigua and Barbuda and Montserrat, declared their intention to give urgent consideration to joining in the Accord.

The establishment of the Caribbean Community will see the achievement of an aspiration that began in December, 1965, at Dickenson Bay, Antigua, when the governments of Antigua and Barbuda, Barbados and Guyana signed an agreement to establish a Caribbean Free Trade Area. During the two years following this agreement, studies were carried out to see how far the liberalisation of trade could be linked with other regional efforts to promote the development of the area. This culminated in crucial decisions being taken at the 1967 Heads of Government Conference in Barbados. The Conference not only endorsed the framework of the Dickenson Bay Agreement, but also accepted a number of positive proposals designed to carry the regional movement beyond the limited strategy of a free trade area.

The Heads of Government enumerated areas where a regional effort would be likely to allow greater benefits to accrue to the area. Indeed, these were set out specifically in Annex A to the CARIFTA

(Caribbean Free Trade Association) Agreement, indicating that the regional association was intended to be a dynamic institution. Thus the Annex anticipated a Common External Tariff, a programme for the location of industries in the Less Developed Countries, a regional policy on the granting of incentives to industry, marketing arrangements for an agreed list of agricultural commodities and the establishment of regional sea and air carriers, among other things.

The CARIFTA Agreement came into effect on May 1, 1968, and by August 1968 covered the following territories: Antigua, Barbados, Dominica, Grenada, Guyana, Jamaica, Montserrat, St Kitts-Nevis-Anguilla, St Lucia, St Vincent and Trinidad and Tobago. In May 1971, Belize (British Honduras) became a member.

Successive meetings of the CARIFTA Council of Ministers and of the Heads of Government grappled with the problem of further economic integration and functional co-operation. After five years of in-depth studies, of deliberations and of bargaining, the Seventh Heads of Government Conference of October 1972 took the decisions to establish a Caribbean Community embracing efforts at economic integration, but also including the co-ordination of foreign policy and the institutionalisation of existing areas of functional co-operation.

The Caribbean Community will have as its principal organs the Conference of Heads of Government and the Common Market Council. As institutions of the Community, there will be a number of Standing Committees of Ministers. Associated institutions will also be recognised.

An integral feature of the Caribbean Common Market will be the establishment of a Common External Tariff and Common Protective Policy which Barbados, Guyana, Jamaica and Trinidad and Tobago agreed to adopt with effect from 1st August, 1973, as between themselves. Members of this House are aware that by virtue of some aspects of my recent Budgetary proposals, Barbados will already have begun to meet its obligations under the Community Treaty.

The governments, parties to the Accord, also agreed to establish a Caribbean Investment Corporation, to apply an agreement for the Harmonisation of Fiscal Incentives, and to conclude a Double Taxation Treaty by the 1st June, 1973. The three relevant instruments have already been signed by the Minister of External Affairs.

Another measure provided for is the elaboration of a scheme for the Rationalisation of Agriculture in the region, to be introduced by 1st July, 1973.

The Community and Common Market are intended to promote the co-ordinated development of the region and to increase intra-regional trade thereby reducing dependence on extra-regional sources. The community will institutionalise the machinery for the many shared services, which already exist and which even the most prosperous of the More Developed Countries, could not operate on its own. Moreover, the region as a whole will carry more bargaining weight when confronting third countries, trading groups and international organisations.

In order to reap the benefits that the new Community and Common Market offer, Barbadian businessmen – indeed regional businessmen –must undertake a re-examination of the needs of the area and structure their production lines to meet these needs.

The Common Market should provide an opportunity for our industrial and agricultural sectors to leap forward. With the necessary determination, the region's economy can become vibrant within a relatively short period of time.

This government has constantly recognised the desirability of developing closer relationships with the other English-speaking Caribbean territories – not only because of our similar historical, cultural and economic background, but also because of the need to protect our small communities from exploitation by undesirable influences. I need hardly remind honourable members that only two years ago, the Governor-General stated in his Throne Speech:

'My Government will continue to play an active role in the attainment of economic integration in the Commonwealth Caribbean. In particular, no effort will be spared to ensure that satisfactory decisions are reached on such important matters as the harmonisation of fiscal incentives, the rationalisation of agriculture and the location of industries.'

And so the package contained in the Community Treaty places high priority on the strengthening of the economies of the Westindian territories. Within the framework of this Community and the Common Market lies the opportunity for greater and more rapid economic development for the area.

I propose to join with the Heads of Government of Guyana, Jamaica, and Trinidad and Tobago and sign the Community Treaty at Chaguaramas, Trinidad and Tobago on 4th July, 1973, the anniversary of the birth of the late Norman Washington Manley. When the Community Treaty has been ratified in accordance with our constitutional procedure, that Treaty and all other relevant instruments will be laid on the table in both Houses of Parliament.

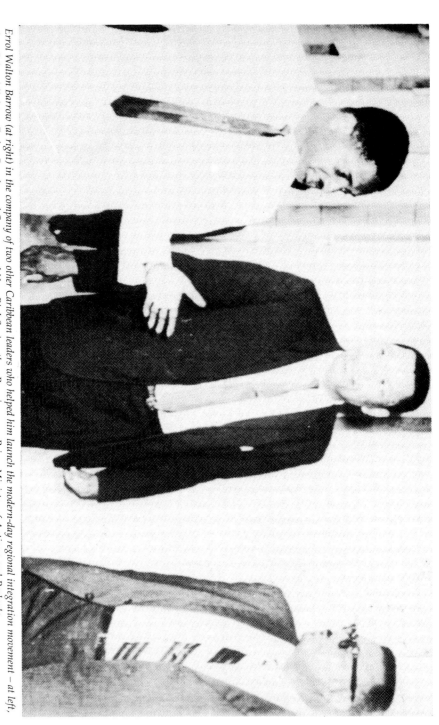

Errol Walton Barrow (at right) in the company of two other Caribbean leaders who helped him launch the modern-day regional integration movement – at left, then Prime Minister, Forbes Burnham of Guyana, and Vere Bird Senior, then Premier, now Prime Minister of Antigua and Barbuda. Barbados, Guyana and Antigua and Barbuda, under the leadership of these men, launched the Caribbean Free Trade Area (CARIFTA), the precursor of the Caribbean Community, now a 13-nation economic grouping, stretching from Belize and Jamaica in the north to Guyana and Trinidad and Tobago in the south.

"A giant step for all of us"

Address at the signing ceremony of the Treaty of Chaguaramas establishing the Caribbean Community and Common Market (CARICOM). Chaguaramas, Trinidad. July 4, 1973

Your Excellencies,
Distinguished guests,
Comrades and friends,

To those who have not been engaged upon the slow process of Caribbean integration, it would appear that this journey commenced at Chaguaramas a few short months ago, and like a race which takes place in a stadium, the end is where the start was.

But the process, as far as three of us, I would say all of us here, certainly the four Prime Ministers, are concerned, goes a long way further back than that.

To the Chairman of this meeting, and the distinguished Prime Minister of Trinidad and Tobago, it started with his struggles at the University of Oxford, when I can truly say, he wrestled with the beast at Ephesus. That chapter in his life has not really been written, but some of us are aware that those who would distort the whole course of Westindian history set out to thwart the attempts of our distinguished Prime Minister of Trinidad and Tobago, to put the Westindian history in its proper perspective, and to give new hope to the people who had been subjected to colonial tutelage for such a long time.

I think that the writings of Dr Williams, the economic researches of Professor Arthur Lewis, were the first faint glimmerings of the indication that the Caribbean people, were capable of managing their own affairs.

We have been a people who have been imbued with a sense of our own inadequacy. Half a generation later, the Prime Minister of Jamaica, who is on this platform, the Prime Minister of Guyana who is on my left, and I, under the leadership of the Prime Minister of

Guyana, who was the President of the first Westindian association founded in the United Kingdom, that was the Westindian Student's Union; we staged the first public meeting on Caribbean integration in the United Kingdom, and we followed the biblical injunction by staging that meeting in the lion's den itself; in that bastion of imperialism which is described as Trafalgar Square.

A lot of our fellow Westindians were rather amazed at our temerity, and we solicited the assistance of our colleagues from other parts of the world in making a bold stand on the need for Westindian integration. I should like to pay tribute to the President of the Westindian Students Union – the first President, the former President, my colleague, Mr Linden Forbes Sampson Burnham, on having the courage and the foresight to lead us on these bold excursions which we followed from time to time, in protesting against conditions in the Westindies, and indeed, supporting our comrades from Africa and other parts of the colonial empires in their protests against the conditions under which our people suffered.

Occasions for making disclosures of this kind are not frequent. I can now disclose that it was on the 4th July, 1965, that the Prime Minister of Guyana met with me in Barbados, at my invitation to discuss the possibility of establishing a free trade area between our two countries in the first instance, and the rest of the Caribbean at such time as they would be ready to follow our example.

The letter which I wrote was in my own fine Barbadian hand which is sometimes illegible. But apparently, the Prime Minister of Guyana was able to read that letter, because of his, he informs me, Barbadian ancestry. Therefore, the hieroglyphics were not entirely strange to him.

That letter must for some time remain in the archives of the Prime Minister of Guyana because I had a few rather caustic observations to make about the failure of our people to get together in some meaningful kind of association. I regret to say that in typical style, a style which has not been unassociated with my posture either in the courts of law or legislative councils, I had some rather personal statements to make about the failure of our leaders to get together in a meaningful association.

So we have for the moment to draw a veil of secrecy and silence over the contents, or the full contents, of that letter. One day, about 25 years after we have both of us relinquished voluntarily the positions which we now hold, the archivist may be given permission for the sake of future generations to publish the full contents of that letter.

In that letter, I invited the Prime Minister of Guyana to come to Barbados so that we could hold these discussions and today, I am very happy to be here, some eight years later to be a signatory to the documents for whose signing we have been summoned by the distinguished Prime Minister of Trinidad and Tobago.

To me it is the end of a long journey. Neither one of us, either the Prime Minister of Jamaica, the Prime Minister of Guyana, or I, had any ambitions to be Prime Ministers. We had ambitions at that time, to see the Caribbean integrated. Today I hear the young aspiring political contenders stating that they want to be Prime Ministers as if being a Prime Minister is like taking an examination and once you achieve the pass mark you are automatically a Prime Minister.

I remember well that in 1955, if I may reminisce very, very shortly, that the General Secretary of the Barbados Workers' Union and the late Norman Washington Manley, whose birthday we commemorate today, and I hope the Prime Minister of Trinidad and Tobago will forgive me for making reference to this, spent two days trying to persuade the Prime Minister of Trinidad and Tobago that he must take his rightful place on the Caribbean political scene.

This is another illustration of the statement which I made a few moments ago that none of the three of us set out to be Prime Ministers. I can now say that remembering what took place in Kingston, Jamaica, none of the four of us set out to be Prime Ministers. The distinguished Prime Minister of Trinidad and Tobago did not even want to be a politician.

So that today when I hear criticism of leadership in the Caribbean, those criticisms would probably have been justified, and justifiably levelled at some of our predecessors in office; but they certainly cannot be levelled against any of the four heads of governments here who have been dragged reluctantly to the high offices which we now occupy.

I hope that when the time comes that we will not be dragged reluctantly from those high offices which we now occupy. The problem which confronts the Westindian people today, is one of persuasion, to persuade people of the calibre of the Prime Minister of Trinidad and Tobago and other distinguished people who have contributed towards the success of this experiment to remain with us and to make a further contribution so that our countries will be able to progress not because of any predilections on our part to preside over the destinies of our peoples, but it will be dependent upon the willingness of the people of the Westindies to recognise the quality and the nature of the leadership which some of our countries enjoy, and that does not necessarily include Barbados, but it does not necessarily exclude Barbados either.

So, Mr Chairman, it was on the 4th July, 1965 one small step for two countries. Today as a signatory to this agreement, I should like to paraphrase the words of Mr Neil Armstrong[*] and say it is a giant step for all of us.

[*]The first American astronaut to walk on the moon.

Speaking for the confraternity of pain and deprivation

Address to the 29th Annual Governors' Meeting of the World Bank and International Monetary Fund (IMF) in Washington, D.C., 3 October, 1974.

I have the distinctive honour to address this meeting on behalf of the Governors of the Bank for the Bahamas, Guyana, Jamaica and Trinidad and Toabago, as well as for my own country, Barbados, and if they should so wish the rest of the Caribbean Community not represented here at this Twenty-Ninth Annual Meeting of the International Monetary Fund and of the World Bank.

I should like to congratulate Mr McNamara (Robert)[*] for his very constructive and thought-provoking speech to us and for the efforts which he and the Executive Board extended on behalf of us all in the developing world during this past year. The institutional developments relating to the World Bank Group and specifically the Development Committee, which we support, should provide material assistance to the Group in the years ahead and enable it to achieve the realistic goals which it has set for itself.

Since the meeting in Nairobi last year developments in the international economy have introduced new financial crises and have placed additional obstacles in the way of developing countries as they strive to provide more jobs and improve the standard of living of their peoples. We in the Commonwealth Caribbean have not escaped these convulsions; and we are striving, through regional co-operation as well as through our own individual efforts, not only to meet the present difficulties, but also to provide for the necessary long-term restructuring of our economies. But in these efforts, we require the full support of the international institutions and particularly the World Bank Group.

We believe that if the international institutions are to play their expected role in the modern world they must work with the support and the efforts of the peoples in the developing world; they must

[*] Then President of the World Bank.

encourage them through financial and technical support to redouble their efforts and so provide more jobs, more school places, better health facilities, more houses, and a more diversified production structure than would otherwise have been possible. But the relationship between the World Bank group and the developing countries can be productive only if it is conceived in terms of a partnership at the highest; but more properly as principals working through an agency for the fulfilment of the collective and individual objectives of the members of the organisation.

We in the Commonwealth Caribbean welcome constructive comments and advice on the policies we pursue and on the methods of introducing feasible modifications. We recognise that the World Bank Group can bring to bear on our development problem advice and experience drawn from a wide cross section of the developing world. At the same time, since development is about people and for people, development processes work only through the institutions and systems that have become part of the country's way of life; and they will work only if the people are satisfied that they respond to their real needs and circumstances. In this sensitive area, therefore, the views and practices of the recipient countries cannot be lightly ignored or, worse still, discarded. It is the antithesis of co-operation and counter-productive in the extreme for the World Bank Group to impose as preconditions for its support, policies which we in these countries are convinced are inappropriate or impossible to implement at any particular point in time. What clearly is necessary is for a continuing dialogue, without preconditions, between the World Bank Group and the client country through which an acceptable package of policies and financial support can be worked out. The World Bank Group must accept as a fact that the government and people of a country are most concerned about their own future and fully realise that the primary responsibility for achieving the highest rate of economic development rests on themselves. But in this they need the support of the institutions based on effective consultation.

This need for continuing dialogue has always been necessary. But it is even more necessary now as we in the Caribbean strive to cope with the development problem complicated by the energy crisis. These circumstances call for the closest possible co-operation and genuine sympathy from the World Bank Group. It is, therefore, disturbing to us to find that, in the current aggravated circumstances that we face, the World Bank Group seeks to impose preconditions for its support which are unattainable even in normal times. To give an example, the high imported inflation from which we all suffer calls for special measures to assist the lowest income groups. This must affect the level of public savings. Quite clearly, we must find intolerable, a precondition which imposes on us a level of public sector savings unattainable even in the absence of such pressures. A similar situation arises in respect of our public utilities, severely affected by the higher prices for oil, machinery and equipment. If they are required to achieve the same rate of return as before, even when they are adding to their fixed assets, then they too will add to internal inflation. But how can the underemployed rural dweller absorb higher utility charges when he is already burdened with higher prices for rice, flour and meat? Yet measures such as these, including completely new concepts relating to credit worthiness, are being imposed on some developing countries as preconditions for Bank assistance. If these measures are insisted upon there can be only one result – the destruction of the social fabric and cohesiveness in the societies which will make any form of development impossible.

This is why we emphasise the need for constructive dialogue. We believe that the World Bank Group must always be guided by the spirit of its Charter which emphasises the role of the Group as agents in the development process. Such a role is inconsistent with the adoption of preconceived policies and concepts which are insensitive to the real problems that we in the developing countries face.

If, as we hope and should believe, the Bank really wants to assist us, the small developing countries with special problems, then a special approach is clearly necessary. I have referred to the need for dialogue. There is also the need for special measures to speed up the disbursement of the Bank's assistance. We are mindful of the strictures in the Bank's Articles of Agreement, which limit the extent to which non-project lending can be undertaken. We are also aware, and we appreciate, the excellence of the Bank's project preparation work and the contribution which this can make to financial discipline and institution building in small developing countries such as our own. Nevertheless, we believe that the pressures which the present situation creates for an early transfer of real resources on the scale required and within the time period necessary cannot be effected solely through project lending. If the Bank is to be effective a much greater proportion of its resources must be disbursed in the form of programme loans to accelerate economic and social development and make an early contribution to the creation of jobs.

There is a further reason why programme lending must be adopted in dealing with small developing countries such as our own. Many of the projects which we have are small and discreet, but they all add up to a development programme which has meaning to our population. The Bank can assist us in meaningful ways only if it adapts its policies to suit the special circumstances that we face. Regrettably, this is not now the case.

One of the ways in which the World Bank Group can adapt its policies to meet our special circumstances is to provide additional assistance through our Caribbean Development Bank. However, in using the regional institution to channel World Bank funds, two important guidelines must be observed. First, such assistance as is provided through the regional financial institutions, should be supplementary to, and not at the expense of the other financial and technical support, coming directly from the Bank to its members; in other words, the Caribbean Development Bank should be used as a vehicle for increasing the financial assistance which the Bank will provide for countries in the Commonwealth Caribbean. I wish to emphasise, as Chairman of the Board of Governors, that the Caribbean Development Bank should not be regarded as an alternative vehicle for providing the same amount of support. Second, in providing through the Caribbean Development Bank the World Bank should not impose criteria and restrictions which would inhibit the regional institution and make it ineffective as a vehicle for transmitting such support. Assistance should always be provided on the most concessionary terms in order to meet the needs of the poorest countries of the region.

The financial crisis in which the small developing countries of the Caribbean are now being tempestuously tossed around adds new urgency to questions which we have raised in the past – one of these is the introduction of third window[**] in the Bank. We are not unmindful of the problem of finding additional resources which could be made available on special concessionary terms. We do, however, feel that when all of us are recoiling from the special problems of imported inflation and the general problems of underdevelopment, then the needs of all of us, and not only a few of us, in the developing world must be taken into account. It may well be that an essential prerequisite for mobilising the resources required will be a restructuring of the shareholding in the Bank to reflect the realities of the circumstances that face us today and of the special position of the oil producing countries in particular. There is in our view no justification for the international community not facing up to this issue.

[**] 'Third Window' refers to the lending section of the bank. A first window might represent, for example, loans at ordinary, i.e. non-concessionary rates, while a second window offered easier terms.

106

We propose that special devices be adopted now to alleviate the heavy debt burden that the developing country clients of the Bank now bear. This burden is now critical; it will become increasingly so in the light of the current excessively high borrowing rates. We, therefore, propose for consideration, the establishment of a compensatory tranche*** of soft funds to alleviate this burden on developing countries whose development efforts are being threatened by burdensome debt service payments. We are prepared to submit a detailed formulation of this proposal to the Bank.

We acknowledge that under the dynamic leadership of Mr McNamara, the Bank has discarded many of the shibboleths that formerly impaired the quality of the assistance it provided in the overall development effort. This evolution must continue and the Bank, recognising the principles of national sovereignty over natural resources, must play a constructive and positive role in ensuring that countries with such resources obtain the best possible returns, measured in national terms, from those assets which they are fortunate to have.

The Bank can assist in a number of ways. Firstly, by financing the infrastructure required for the exploitation of these resources. Secondly, by participating directly in the financing of natural resource projects and in assisting developing countries in negotiating the best possible terms in their exploitation; and third, by invoking the powers provided in the Articles of Agreement of the World Bank to guarantee market loans raised by the developing countries for participation in the projects themselves. We are convinced that through these devices the Bank can make a signal contribution to international economic stability and development and enable small countries to obtain a fair and just return from their national assets.

I should now like to make a few observations on behalf of the government of Barbados and based largely upon my personal experience.

As with most institutions, whether international or governmental, that may owe allegiance to several masters the International Bank for Reconstruction and Development has developed a personality of its own which does not necessarily bear resemblance to the demeanours, physiognomies, or outlooks of all or any of its members; and what is probably more alarming, the Bank has developed a will of its own which more frequently than not, fails to reflect the individual will and

---

*** 'Tranche' refers to the reserve of money contributed to the institution and then available for on-lending to members.

aspirations of any of its members, or the collective will of all as concluded in the annual statements of the Governors or in the resolutions which we may pass from time to time.

Like most bureaucracies, the Bank has developed its own theology with accompanying ritual of canons and liturgy and its own hierarchy of saints and priests and novices. We the Governors are expected to attend the celebration of the mass on the saint days which usually extend over the last week in September and first week in October, dependent, for all intents and purposes, on the phases of the moon.

I am aware that the Bank was designed to engineer the reconstruction and development of the European countries which had been devastated by World War II. In that regard the Bank succeeded in restoring the mighty to their seat, without having to worry itself morally or otherwise with exalting the humble and meek.

In its preoccupation with what it considered to be its prime objective of restoration, it not only restored the gap between the rich and the poor, but by accident rather than by design continued to exacerbate the growing economic disharmonies between the absolute rich and, what has been described at this very meeting, as the absolute poor.

We in the Caribbean are not classified by this or by any other international institution among the congregation of the absolute poor.

Our countries do not figure among those selected for redemption because we have managed by our own efforts to raise the per capita incomes of our peoples and because we have succeeded in developing our health and educational services to levels which frequently equate, and sometimes surpass, those of more prosperous countries.

We have done so despite the low prices hitherto paid for our primary products and despite the lack of encouragement and assistance from the countries which constituted our traditional trading partners. We have been imbued not with righteousness but with hopelessness, but we have managed to muster our courage to take our destinies into our own hands.

I speak for the median minority; for those hitherto silent members who have come out of great tribulations but who recognise the soul-destroying tribulations of those who are still members of the confraternity of pain and deprivation. These are the one billion persons to whom Mr McNamara referred who suffocate and suffer with per capita incomes of less than $200 per annum.

We come from the Caribbean not as supplicants at the gate – the gates of the IDA[****] have long been shut in our faces – but as members of the co-operative anxious to do business and with bankable assurances.

It is at this stage that the inquisition begins. And after the inquisition, a period of instruction on how we should amend our wicked, wicked ways of trying to overcome unemployment and raise our living standards. We must do penance on our knees, create more unemployment, devalue our currencies, freeze wages at levels which are demonstrably below subsistence in order to preserve our comparitive costs advantages, and read the economic sermons of the Reverend Dr Malthus[*****] in all our churches twice a day at matins and vespers and four times on a Sunday.

If I appear to be critical of the current policies pursued by the World Bank Group, it is not because I am unaware of the important strides which the Bank has made over the past several years and of the dynamic plans that it proposes for the five years ahead. We in the Caribbean are pleased to support the adoption of the proposal for a lending programme of US $36 billion over the period 1974-78, a programme which, in our view, calls not only for increased borrowing by the Bank but also for an increase in capital subscription. Our comments derive entirely from the fact that we are inordinately dependent on the international institutions for our economic viability, and for the preservation of our independence; we, therefore, feel compelled to urge this important institution to adapt its policies and programmes to meet the specific circumstances which we face, so that the assistance which it can provide to us will produce the results which both we and the Bank expect, sufficiently and in time.

[****]IDA is the International Development Association, an institution of the World Bank which specialises in providing soft loans to developing countries.

[*****] "Rev. Dr Malthus" is a reference to Robert Thomas Malthus (1766-1834), a British economist best known for his warning that unless world population growth was controlled it would outstrip world food supply.

Co-operation to survive
and advance

Address to the Annual Governors' Meeting of the
Caribbean Development Bank (CDB), held in
Barbados on 26 May, 1975.

Your Excellencies,
Fellow Governors and Advisers,
Mr President,
and Directors of the Caribbean Development Bank,
Distinguished Guests and Observers,
Ladies and Gentlemen,

The normal procedure at these Annual Meetings of the Bank is for the Chairman of the Board of Governors to invite the Head of Government of the host country to welcome the visitors and to declare the meeting open. There is then a vote of thanks and the Prime Minister leaves, after which the Chairman of the Board of Governors delivers his report and the more practical aspect of the Board's business is embarked upon with the President's address.

This year, Providence has ordained that you should be spared at least three of these addresses, but nevertheless, it is still my duty and pleasure as Chairman of the Cabinet of Barbados to say welcome to you all. As Chairman of the Board of Governors of the Bank, I should like to say a special word of welcome to the representatives of the Republic of Colombia, which is being represented at the Board of Governors Meeting for the first time since being admitted to full membership and, happily for us, by a long established friend of the Caribbean, the distinguished Dr Carlos Sanz de Santamaria.

I should also like to record with pleasure the presence, as observers from our neighbours in the Caribbean, of Sr. Julio Imperatori, Vice President of the Banco Nacional de Cuba, Sr. Andres Julio Espinal of the Central Bank of the Dominican Republic, Sr. Luis E. Agrait and others from the Commonwealth of Puerto Rico; Sr. Wenceslas Salas of the Bank of Mexico; Mr Braam of the Ministry of Finance of

Surinam and also His Excellency E.O. Kolade, the High Commissioner of Nigeria to many CARICOM countries.

In every respect, with all respect, and in my multiple capacities – welcome.

I have no intention of leaving the meeting at this stage, neither will I permit a vote of thanks.

It is my sincere wish that you are by now quite certain of your welcome to our friendly island. I say this, not only because I know the people of Barbados wish it to be so, but because it is important that we should be sufficiently composed to reflect, for the next day or two, on the course travelled by this important regional institution during the past year, and to set its course, together, for the year ahead or more. Occasions like these are important and necessary if we are not to feel, with justification, that we are but the victims of events and institutions alike, rather than the framers in large measure of our destiny and our fate. This is our Bank, and if we would have it serve us, we must first serve it.

In my view, it is timely to remind ourselves that this institution was created, not so much to fulfil some hallowed and time-bound concept of development, nor the dream of one visionary or another, but to foster and contribute to the improvement in the welfare and living conditions of the peoples of the region. The precise methods by which this goal of human upliftment is accomplished may, and indeed must, vary with time and circumstances. But the goal itself cannot change.

The Annual Report of the Directors reminds us that recent developments in the wider world around us have made attainment of our goal more difficult rather than easier. For many years, instability and uncertainty have been the main features of the international financial and monetary system. This has been followed by inflation and shortages – especially in food and energy. Recession and growing unemployment now threaten to overshadow the severity and seriousness of the former crises. Because of this it is perhaps understandable, though not necessarily excusable, that more attention would appear to be given to individual survival, rather than to international co-operation and development. Our responsibility in the developing world is to continue to remind the international community that the transfer of resources from areas of relative abundance to areas of relative scarcity and need, is not only a social and economic, but the moral and practical imperative of our times.

This Bank, like others of its kind, was created to assist the transfer of resources to this region as well as the re-distribution of resources within the region. I am particularly encouraged by two recent developments which, among others, give clear evidence of the continued success of the Bank in attracting resources to the Region. I refer to the interest expressed by General (Yakabu) Gowon, President of the Republic of Nigeria, in channelling funds to the region through the Bank, and the re-affirmation of a decision by the Governors of the Inter-American Development Bank to make funds available fo the Caribbean Development Bank for on-lending to all member countries, whether or not members of the Inter-American Development Bank.

The loan by the government of Trinidad and Tobago on soft terms to assist the LDCs (Lesser Developed Countries) in providing counterpart funds for projects financed by the Bank, and the creation by the government of Venezuela of a Trust Fund in the Bank are without a doubt our most outstanding examples to date of use of the Bank to redistribute resources within the region.

I need hardly remind you that this effort to attract resources is crucial to the success of the Bank, and that we must individually and collectively pursue policies that will make the attraction and distribution of resources a continuingly successful exercise.

A review of the activities of the Bank during the past year reminds us, however, that development, even when aided by indigenous institutions and inspired by native genius, is a complex process requiring sustained effort and the tackling of many different problems simultaneously. Resources, scarce and necessary though they are, are by our own experience more difficult to disburse than to mobilise. The Annual Report reminds us yet again that disbursement of resources is our least distinguished accomplishment. Some member countries, like my own, are even less distinguished in this regard than most. Because of this I might perhaps venture a few observations on this recurring and vexing problem.

It is a widely held view, though perhaps not as widely expressed, that loan disbursement procedures appear to be designed not just to safeguard the interest of the lender, but to tax the ingenuity of the borrower. (For my part I remain convinced that they are designed to tax the ingenuity of the lender as well!) Much can and is being done by the Bank to improve and simplify its disbursement procedures. But as has been observed before by the Bank and its borrowers alike, what is done in this direction must always be consistent with maintaining the integrity and viability of the institution itself. It is, after all – however regrettable member countries find it – a loan institution. The maxim 'Neither a borrower nor a lender be' is not emblazoned on the escutcheon of the Bank.

It is recognised too that disbursement is as much a function of lending procedures as of the absorptive capacity of borrowers. Generally, though not invariably, lower absorptive capacity is associated with low levels of development. Unsuitable and inadequate institutional arrangements, fiscal constraints and scarcity of skilled manpower all contribute to the inablility of our countries to absorb financing at the rates that we would wish. It is clear that these bottlenecks must be tackled vigorously and conscientiously if we are to succeed, and the Bank with us and through us. In my view there are a number of things that can be done now to reduce these obstacles to disbursement.

Firstly, there is training in appropriate project skills of persons whose jobs it will be to formulate and implement projects. I would urge your support then for the proposed Project Training Courses at the Centre for Development Studies with the assistance of the Bank and under the supervision of our former President, Sir Arthur Lewis who has consented to be the Centre's Director. Shortage of skilled and experienced project specialists is a universal, not just a regional, phenomenon. This alone would suggest that we should attempt to develop these skills here in the Region with the assistance of this our own financing institution, the Caribbean Development Bank.

Secondly, the process of identification and formulation of viable regional projects must continue. We have made an encouraging start in this direction, but it is only a start. Those who are impatient with results in this area to date, should reflect on the complexity of the exercise and the cost to the region, should adequate research and preparation not precede implementation.

Thirdly, I turn to the thorny problem of institutional reform. Here the problem of skilled manpower shortages confronts us again. More important than this, however, is the question of political will. The dismantling and reform of institutions invariably involves tampering with vested interests of one kind or another. All institutions, however efficient, serve some purpose and some interests – though not always the right ones. Experience would suggest that the tackling of this problem is necessary to our success in raising the living standards of the broad mass of our people. We neglect it at great costs and to our own peril.

I observed earlier that the temptation is perhaps for some, especially the relatively better off, to avoid co-operative effort and pursue individual survival. In this way some or a few might indeed survive. It is unlikely that any of us would advance. Ever-widening co-operative efforts are called for now more than ever. Our problems no longer come singly, as we know only too well from recent experience with inflation and recession.

We must strengthen the inner circles in order to survive.

We must strengthen the inner circles in order to survive and move to wider circles of regional co-operation, if we are to hold our own in this era of crisis and strain.

We must strengthen the inner circles in order to survive; move to wider circles of regional co-operation if we are to hold our own; and press on to ever-widening circles of international co-operation if we are to concern ourselves not merely with survival and keeping up with the rest, but with the advancement and relentless onward march of the people whom we claim to represent and who expect us, through this institution, to show them clearly the way ahead.

Prime Minister Errol Barrow (fifth from right), visits the site of the headquarters of the Caribbean Development Bank (CDB), east of Bridgetown, during the construction phases in the early 1970s.

Mr Barrow was one of the early proponents of the formation of the CDB, and defended its role as one of the primary channels of international aid into the Caribbean, and as an important institution to promote regional self-reliance.

Bank President, Mr William Demas is second from right.

Prime Minister, Errol Barrow (second from right), poses with two Canadian government officials (extreme left and right), and close personal friend, Carlton Braithwaite, at the Paris Air Show in the mid-1970s. Mr Barrow was himself a fully qualified pilot, and saw active service in the Second World War as a flying officer in the Royal Air Force.

Prime Minister Errol Walton Barrow personally oversees work at the new international airport building in Barbados, just before his Democratic Labour Party (DLP) lost office in the summer of 1976.
Project Manager Rudy Matthews (gesticulating), points out aspects of the project to Mr Barrow, (third from right).
The new terminal building was opened in 1979.

"Development and Democracy"

Anniversary lecture to the Democratic Labour Party's Academy of Politics on 25 April, 1980

What is democracy? The word is a combination of two Greek words DEMOS (People) and KRATEIN (to rule). In other words, rule by the people either directly or through elected representatives, as distinct from rule by a person, a monarch, a king, an emperor, a dictator, an oligarchy, or a few people – rule then by the majority.

I should like to make my language unambiguous from the outset by saying that democracy as most political scientists understand the term, is not a philosophy in itself nor a body of beliefs on which one can simply pin abiding faith by declaring I believe in democracy and done with that. All you have established is a commitment to a system in arriving at decisions but not the nature of the decisions themselves nor the criteria by which they may have to be evaluated.

The democratic process is supposed to ensure that the decisions which are made, enure to the benefit of the greatest number and that there is some substantial support for actions and programmes embarked upon in the name of the people. Development is described in the 'New World' Dictionary as economic, social and political progress after emergence into statehood.

The terms have been most frequently used internationally with reference to Third World countries and specifically we have had the Development Decade and the United Nations Conferences on Trade and Development, the Inter-American Development Bank, the Caribbean Development Bank and so on ad infinitum. The government of Puerto Rico named their most successful development institution Fomento. In whatever language, in whatever country, in whatever forum we speak, when we say development, we immediately stimulate the interest of all classes and races and ideologies, the interest of the banker, and baker and candlestick maker, the gluttons, the scholars and even the dunces. There is always the promise in development of something for everyone, a little more for some, a little less for others, rich man, poor man, beggar and thief.

In order to understand the objective of developmental process which, I take it, is to become developed, it is necessary to know what is the antithesis – 'underdeveloped' or 'undeveloped'. Economists and sociologists tend to employ definitions which are mainly concerned with per capita incomes, extent of industrialisation, consumption of electricity, number of telephones, television sets and motor vehicles and other particularly North American criteria which are demonstrably irrelevant to the kind of societies that such humanists as Dr Kenneth Kaunda and Dr Julius Nyerere are trying to reconstruct in their respective countries. Von der Mehd, himself a distinguished American political scientist, had this to say, 'The average American has built a stereotype of an underdeveloped country. According to this stereotype, a state is considered underdeveloped if it cannot be related to a model based upon a Western European or North American polity which is democratic and which has several political parties, widespread literacy, a high standard of living, wide circulation of newspapers and books, consensus on the fundamentals of government, a long history of peace, and (in some models) a white population'.

K. H. Pfeffer of the University of Punjab wrote in 1960, 'The term underdeveloped country is based on the assumption that there exists a commonly accepted standard of development. A person or a group or a nation can only be called underdeveloped when there is general agreement what a developed or a fully developed person, nation or group ought to be like. Thus, the very category underdeveloped should be tested before use, since it is loaded with values and prejudices'.

When I accepted the invitation to deliver this first of the annual Anniversary Lectures, which happily coincides with the celebrations of the 25th Anniversary of the founding of the Democratic Labour Party, I had no idea that the title chosen for this lecture would be one over which I would have had to agonise for such long periods of time or that it would be fraught with so many semantic, philological, and philosophical difficulties. In order to escape from the entanglement of time consuming academic quarrels, I wish to crave your indulgence to allow me to adopt for our own limited purposes some definitions more relevant to the human situation in our own country.

Firstly, I wish you to accept that since 1980 is neither the beginning of creation nor, as far as I can discern, the end of history, that all countries are developing countries and all peoples all over the world are evolving in different ways under different systems towards conditions of perfection or imperfection which human ingenuity at this early dawn in the history of mankind cannot foretell.

Secondly, that for the time being, for lack of better, we as a people, prefer a democratic system of arriving at decisions. The problem of political development, in theory at least, is not one which inhibits us, since we are actors ourselves and not acted upon as we were before independence.

Thirdly, that the development which concerns us all immediately is social and economic in quantity, and personal and human in quality.

And that brings us straight to the examination of the way in which this development is to be achieved and sustained under the democratic process.

On the 15th January, 1941, President Franklin D. Roosevelt delivered these words in his message to the United States Congress: 'The basic things expected by our people of their political and economic system, are simple. They are: Equality of opportunity for youth and others. Jobs for those who can work. Security for those who need it. The ending of special privilege for the few. The preservation of civil liberties for all. The enjoyment of the fruits of scientific progress for a wider and constantly rising standard of living'.

These things cannot come automatically, they must result from an economic relationship in which all (the citizens) have a shared interest and concern.

Article Three of the Constitution of the Democratic Labour Party sets out the objects of the party. Three (b) is to raise the standard of living of the people of Barbados and create the greatest measure of social betterment by sound management of the financial and economic resources of the country. Three (e) is to create and maintain a social and economic atmosphere conducive to the enjoyment of equal opportunities and of the democratic way of life by all.

The founders of the Democratic Labour Party twenty five years ago and the President of the United States of America forty years ago, both spoke clearly about equality of opportunity for people. Real equality and real opportunity must open the door to real personal and real human development. Not the kind of opportunity calling at 8.15 a.m.* for requirements and qualifications with which our educational system has not provided the average citizen. I respectfully submit that these government programmes have been systematically designed to give the impression that opportunities for employment are

*This is a reference to a government-sponsored short radio programme advertising training and job opportunities.

being created by a government which is in fact, doing nothing more than disseminating advertisements clipped for the most part, from bulletins and information sheets of overseas organisations.

President Franklin D Rooselvelt, the product of a wealthy American capitalist family, speaking to a Congress dominated by the concept of unbridled capitalism and the inestimable benefits of the free enterprise system, did not apologise for stating unequivocally that the first basic that the people expected of their political and economic system was –'Equality of opportunity for youth and others'. How else can people develop? The Gross Domestic Product of a country at factor costs, or market value can grow from year to year. Yet people can stagnate, suffer and succumb. 'Ill fares the land to hastening ills a prey, where wealth accumulates and men decay'.

We in Barbados tend to take cover and run for shelter as soon as the C.Gs, D.Ds, E.L.C.** and the other cohorts of unbridled capitalism deliver their periodic attacks on the principle of socialism which they little understand but feel it their duty to assail.

When he was Chief Minister of Jamaica in the fifties, the late Norman Washington Manley said, 'What is the essence of socialism? It was never put better than by Professor Arthur Lewis when he said with stark simplicity, Socialism is about equality. A socialist believes that the purpose of human history is to achieve a society dominated, dominated, dominated by the concept of equality'.

After all that is what FDR says the people expect of their political system. And he was not speaking about Czechoslovakia or the Union of Soviet Socialist Republics. He was speaking about the broad masses of registered Republicans and registered Democrats living in the free enterprise capitalistic United States of America. This concept of equality – Mr Manley went on – involves a society where the exploitation implicit in the class system has ceased. A society where there is equal opportunity, not (merely) opportunity, but truly equal opportunity for all to share in a rich and varied life and to develop the many and varied solid talents of the human individual. That is development.

Secondly, a society where each person will have equal access to the essential human freedoms, and this involves a society rooted in economic and social security consciously maintained and reinforced by creative human effort, foresight and skill and, lastly, a society where there will be equality of status without which the belief in the supreme significance of the individual is meaningless and largely

**C.Gs, D.Ds are regualr pro-American letter writers to local newspapers. ELC is the pseudonym of former newspaper proprietor Jimmy Cozier, who has a column in the local press.

hypocrisy.

As we enter the decade of the eighties, there is no need for us to contrive new formulae or spin out new high-sounding phrases in an attempt to attract support to our basic philosophy. We leave it to others of baser metal to indulge in calculated political chicanery and to attempt to suborn and subvert the public purpose. True personal development cannot take place if the political leaders of a country believe that the masses are there for manipulation. The Brazilian educator, Paulo Freire wrote, 'A real humanist can be identified more by his trust in the people which engage him in their struggle, than by a thousand actions in their favour without that trust'.

The distribution of largesse which the 'Larousse' English dictionary describes as the distribution of gifts by a superior to inferiors cannot be development. Conspicuous consumption by politicians, particularly undertaken at the expense of the taxpayers, is not development. The construction of office buildings may boost the profits of importers of builders' hardware and provide some jobs at a low technological level in a short time span, but it is not development. The purchase of warships and armoured cars is not development, particularly when no local skills have been mobilised in their acquisition, also at public expense. Gambling is not development. The perpetuation of the persistent poverty of military agriculture, in idealising the plantation system, is not development. The denial of the right to work, the right to eat and even the right to life cannot be development.

It stands to reason that any political party seeking to fulfil the expectations of the populace for equality, jobs, security, the ending of privilege, the preservation of civil liberties and so on, must set about to accomplish these objectives in a planned and organised manner, working along with the people and not in a whimsical opportunistic and patronising manner of which, unfortunately, we see growing manifestations these days. The record of the Democratic Labour Party in fulfilling these objectives has made it possible for real human development to take place.

The elimination of the inequalities of the school fees system and text books, the provision of hot meals, the introduction of National Insurance and social security, severance pay, the systematic expansion of job opportunities through the development of tourism and industry, training in the hotel industry and in the Samuel Jackson Prescod Polytechnic, the Community College, the provision of free university education, the enactment of trade union legislation and tenantry development and control – all of these, and many more too numerous to mention, illustrate that our living has not been in vain.

Let us conclude by summing up Democracy and Development in my terms. Since democracy is rule by the people and in our system, not directly but through elected representatives then the people must tell the representatives and those seeking to represent them what they expect of our political and economic system. Particularly, the young people must be made to feel, however inarticulate they may be, 'right' that someone is prepared to listen to them 'right'. They are tired of being told what they are expected to do. It is time we asked the young people of Barbados how best do you think you can develop as a person, how best can we help you to be creative and to realise to the maximum your human potential.

If I may be allowed to conclude with another quotation from the 'Pedagogy of the Oppressed' by Paulo Freire, 'A revolutionary leadership must practice co-intentional education. Teachers and students (leadership and people) co-intent on reality are both subjects not only in the task of unveiling that reality, and thereby coming to know it critically, but in the task of creating that knowledge. As they attain this knowledge of reality through common reflection and action, they discover themselves, as its permanent recreators. In this way, the presence of the oppressed in the struggle for their liberation will be what it should be, not pseudo participation but committed involvement'.

Errol Walton Barrow stresses a point to journalists at a news conference which he gave while as Leader of the Opposition in the Barbados House of Assembly.

"Begging will not solve our economic problem"

On the Caribbean Basin Initiative (CBI) at a news conference on 22 April, 1982 (abridged version)

I wish to turn, out of a sense of duty, to at least one, probably two or three, of our great Caribbean leaders to disabuse the minds of the public on what Mr (Ronald) Reagan has called, the great Caribbean Basin Initiative (CBI).

My understanding of the English word 'initiative' is something which has been inspired, undertaken, instigated, if you like, put into motion, for the first time by some person or persons.

Therefore, the impression has been spread abroad that the whole concept for an economic plan, if you can dignify it by that name, for the Caribbean area, was initiated either by the President of the United States (Ronald Reagan), by the Prime Minister of Jamaica (Edward Seaga), or by the Prime Minister of Barbados (Tom Adams); and that this initiative with one or two or all three of those persons, is a means of doing something for the benefit of the people of the Caribbean as a whole.

The whole concept of a Caribbean basin was formulated first by the late Dr Eric Williams, Prime Minister of Trinidad and Tobago, in the presence of Dr Willam Demas (the Secretary-General of the Caribbean Community, but now President of the Caribbean Development Bank) and myself, at a private meeting which Dr Williams held at his home, between the three of us in the early '70s.

At that stage we were satisfied that the Caribbean Community was well on its way to becoming an established fact, and Dr Wiliams was looking around to see what further concepts could be initiated for the benefit of the Caribbean region. I remember well sitting around with the two of them, that is the Secretary General of the Caricom Secretariat and the Prime Minister of Trinidad and Tobago and discussing how the region, as a region, can become more integrated.

We had already integrated the Commonwealth Caribbean in the Caribbean Community, that is, all the former British colonies in the

Caribbean and some of the territories which were still British colonies, nearly twice the number that had been members of the ill-fated Federation; had brought them together in an economic grouping.

Dr Williams was a Caribbean integrationist. He had already made overtures to the other Greater Antilles, such as Haiti, the Dominica Republic, Cuba, (about) the idea of eventually embracing them into a wider community. Dr Williams sat down and drew three concentric circles.

The first circle he described as the Caribbean Community, former liberated colonies, now constituting the Caribbean Community. The second concentric circle was the territories in the Caribbean Sea which would include places like Haiti, Santo Domingo, the Antilles – French and Netherlands Antilles. The third circle was the largest, and included all the territories which had coastlines on the Caribbean Sea and the Gulf of Mexico.

If you look at the map behind me, you will see that Guyana is just on the edge. These are the islands including Jamaica; then you have Venezuela and Colombia, which are already members of the Caribbean Development Bank (CDB); then you have Panama, which was formerly part of Colombia; then next to Panama is Costa Rica, Nicaragua, Honduras, Guatemala, Belize and Mexico. Then to the north you have Cuba, Haiti, Santo Domingo, Puerto Rico, and you come all the way down to the American Virgin Islands.

The expression Caribbean Basin countries was one which was formulated. It was formulated in a very restrictive way by Venezuelan publicists earlier in the 50s, as the Venezuelan basin. But, certainly the concept of a Caribbean basin was one which was formulated by Dr Williams and Dr Demas and not by anyone in the United States.

I wish to tell you about a true Caribbean initiative now, because I think we owe it out of respect to the memory of Dr Williams that other people should not try to steal the wonderful ideas which we had for the upliftment of the peoples of the Caribbean, and make us the subject people of other imperialistic powers.

You will notice, gentlemen, that there is a country down here which is called El Salvador. El Salvador is not a Caribbean Basin country. El Salvador is a Pacific country. El Salvador rightly belongs with Japan, and the Philippines, and Hawaii and that group. So if the President of the United States really wanted to do something for the Caribbean, he would not spend half of the money on El Salvador, because $128 million out of $350 million which he is asking the Congress of the United States to appropriate under his Caribbean

Basin Initiative, is for a Pacific country.

But let me go back to the original Caribbean Basin plan. Dr Demas said, we cannot call this wider community, the Caribbean Community; we'll have to look at it from the point of view of the litoral countries.

I want to tell you now of the Caribbean Basin plan. The Caribbean Basin plan asked for no assistance from Great Britain, from the United States of America, from France, from West Germany, from Japan, or any country outside of the Caribbean Basin. It was literally an 'Operation Bootstrap' by which the people of the Caribbean would definitely take over the commanding heights of the economy which President Reagan now wants to hand back to American businessmen.

Dr Williams said that he will spend two thousand million dollars on one project alone. The first project ...

(Journalist, interrupting: "U.S. dollars?")

My recollection is T and T (Trinidad and Tobago) Dollars. When we are in the Caribbean, we do not think of the United States treasury. We were in Port of Spain. So I would have to take it he meant T and T dollars. When I say dollars in Barbados, I do not mean American dollars. I have not become so slave-minded yet.

...Two thousand million dollars which he would find out of Trinidad reserves, in order to build an aluminium refinery if you speak English, aluminum smelter if you speak American, smelter in Trinidad, using Trinidad reserves of natural gas, to process the bauxite which was leaving Jamaica, leaving Suriname, leaving Guyana and going up to places like Kittymack in Canada to be made into aluminum products.

This was the Trinidad government's contribution; no money from the United States; two billion Trinidad and Tobago dollars.

The second thing was that the government of Mexico, at the time the President of Mexico was a gentleman by the name of Alvares Echevarria put forward the idea of a shipping service which would complement the service which we have, and would do all the external shipping for the area.

Let me give you some figures. When I last did a calculation of this two-and-a-half, to three years ago, I calculated that Barbadians were paying $80 million per annum in freight charges to foreign shipping companies. I am sure it is much more than that now, because shipping costs have (gone up) considerably. Let us say around $100 million –Barbados alone. Can you imagine the amount of money that countries like Venezuela, Colombia, Trinidad and Tobago, with heavy equipment, are spending on freight and insurance of goods brought into their countries?

So President Alvares formulated the idea of NUMACAR and asked us to join; that was part of the Caribbean Basin Plan. Unfortunately, I do not think that the present government of Barbaos ever gave very serious consideration to NUMACAR, the external shipping line, because all the statements made by government ministers have been very derogatory, in the same way that all the statements they have been making about the litttle sop that the American Government is throwing at the Eastern Caribbean, have been very adulatory. Anything that is initiated within the region, meets with derision. I think it is a great pity that we do not recognise the talents that we have in the persons like Dr Demas, and Dr Williams and Sir Arthur Lewis, and people of that kind of ability who, in my opinion, have more ability than all the people that they have at the World Bank, International Monetary Fund, put together.

Here was Trinidad offering to put up this money to help the economies of Jamaica, Suriname, and Guyana and to integrate the processing of basic raw materials, because we are always complaining about primary products receiving only low prices, and then our having to pay high prices for manufactured goods coming from the industrial countries.

Here was a great opportunity to industrialise the Westindies. Here was another great opportunity to get control of our shipping. But the efforts of the government of Mexico met with derision, and, recently within the past 12 months, the government of Trinidad and Tobago, has pulled out of the exercise of the international shipping company, for reasons best known to them– but after Dr Williams died. The government of Barbados never really put their hearts and minds in the exercise at all, and they were very easily persuaded by British shipping and British commercial interests, that it is not in our best interest to venture into these deep waters.

The third project which has not got off the ground yet, much to Dr Williams' dismay, he must have died of a broken heart, is the Caribbean Food Plan. Every now and then we read something in the newspaper about the Caribbean Food Plan. We read about the large sums of money which are being spent by all the territories on the import of foodstuffs.

There is no reason why the Caribbean countries, places like St Vincent, Dominica, which claim to be poor countries, and always stretching out their hands asking for money from other people, should not be feeding the whole of the Caribbean and getting money for it, and developing their economies. Dr Williams formulated the idea of the Caribbean Food Plan.

What happens in the Caribbean is that when you have a good idea, either the British or American commercial interests kill the idea or the Westindian governments appoint committee after committee and the experts who sit on these committees, or the civil servants are the main beneficiaries of these well thought out ideas, and spend 15 or 20 years ...

The civil service and British officials and American officials are the main beneficiaries of all our efforts to stimulate economic growth in these countries; too much talking and writing and minutes and that kind of thing.

So the Caribbean Food Plan was the third thrust towards making the region economically self-sufficient.

What I wish to reiterate, for the last time, is that none of these Plans called for any outside expertise, or any outside financial assistance. As a matter of fact, the main rationale of the plan was to make us independent of refineries of aluminium outside, make us independent of external shipping, and make us independent of the imports of food from countries which were outside of the Caribbean.

Now, where did Venezuela come in on this? The Venezuelans, round about 1974, made an offer that they would sell crude oil to the territories at a price of $6.00 per barrel. The price is now $32 per barrel, a barrel is roughly 43-44 gallons. The price in 1972 was round about $1.80, and all the countries were being affected by the OPEC decisions.

The Venezuelans, being members of OPEC, could not break the agreement; so what the Venezuelans said they would do was to give us credit; in other words, we would pay them $6.00 a barrel and, let us say the price was $12 a barrel just for the sake of argument, they would sell us at $6.00 a barrel and the other $6.00 we could use locally for economic development, and it would be a book entry which we would owe the Venezuelan government – theoretically they would owe the Venezuelans this money, but I doubt that the Venezuelan government would ever want to collect that money. There again an initiative coming from within the Caribbean.

You will ask me now, what happened to the plan. It is a very sad story.

Some Foreign ministers got together in New York. I have to speak the truth on this even though I may offend certain people. These Foreign Ministers, having heard about the plan from some of their leaders, like Mr Burnham (Forbes Burnham of Guyana), myself, Dr Williams, and the President of Venezuela, decided that they would summon their own meeting and they invited *Marish and Parish, Sam Cow and Duppy,*[*] everybody. All the OAS (Organisation of American States) people, I believe the Argentinians – they didn't invite the Falkland Islanders – the Chileans, the Salvadoreans, the Ecuadoreans, everybody, because they wanted to get the international spotlight.

(They) held a meeting at the time of the (United Nations) General Assembly in New York, without any authority whatsoever from Dr Williams, the President of Venezuela, or anybody else. At that meeting, they spoke about the Caribbean Basin Plan without anybody telling them to do so. (They) called in the American press, and decided that they were going to have the first meeting in Caracas, Venezuela.

Our understanding between the President of Venezuela, myself, and Dr Williams and Mr Burnham, I believe Mr Manley (Michael Manley, Prime Minister of Jamaica), was that the first meeting was to be held in Port of Spain, since it was Dr Williams' idea; and that Dr Williams would send out the invitations, and that Dr Williams would be chairman of the meeting.

When Dr Williams heard about this meeting which was to be held in Caracas, all hell broke loose, and he said he would have nothing more to do with it. The President of Venezuela sent and called me and asked me to go and speak to Dr Williams and tell Dr Williams that he knew nothing about the meeting which was held in New York; that he had given no one any authority to convene a meeting in Caracas and it was still his understanding that Dr Williams was to send out the invitations; and that the meeting was to be held in Port of Spain under the chairmanship of Dr Williams.

I went to Port of Spain, and I went to see Dr Williams by myself. I explained in great detail to Dr Williams what had happened; how the meeting had been held in New York; who had convened the meeting; their motives for convening the meeting. They meant well, but they wanted to get a little of the limelight, a little of the credit for the Caribbean Basin Plan.

I explained to Dr Williams what the President of Venezuela had told me. Dr Williams sat down for 45 minutes and listened to me, and when I finished speaking, there was a little silence, and he said: 'Have a drink, Errol'. That is the only thing he said for the whole time. He didn't even ask me what I was going to have to drink; he mixed the same thing he was accustomed to drinking which I don't drink, but for politeness, I drank, and that was the end of the

[*]A Barbadian dialect phrase meaning all and sundry.

Caribbean Basin Plan. That's all he said. He didn't even say, as he said on another occasion, 'I dun wid dat.'

Our motto is 'Pride and Industry', and I think that in Barbados we have lost our pride. This is what I particularly want to say: we do not have any pride anymore, because we are joining the ranks of the beggars. We have developed a mendicant mentality, and we are even boasting now of our mendicancy, our success in begging. We have never been a nation of beggars.

I told some American reporters once that I was shocked that countries like Egypt and Israel would have a man like Henry Kissinger (former U.S. Secretary of State) running between their capitals, saying he was making peace. I said that if Henry Kissinger was ever so crazy as to come down to the Caribbean if we ever had any dispute, say with Trinidad and Tobago, that he could be so drunk as to say he was shuttling between Port of Spain and Bridgetown, settling a dispute between Dr Williams and Errol Barrow our people should throw us out of office overnight. We here in the Caribbean should settle our own problems, whether they be political problems, or whether they be economic problems. We do not have any right to our independence, unless we are prepared to settle our economic problems without going cap in hand to other people joining in their sterile ideological disputes, even with some of our own brethren, running cap in hand begging them for money.

No one from outside the region should be able to come in here saying they are settling disputes in the Caribbean. The Caribbean peoples have got to settle their own disputes. If that is alright for Egypt and for the Middle East and for the Israelis, it is because these people want to buy a lot of sophisticated armaments to kill one another, and, therefore, they have to be dependent on the United States, and, therefore, they have to suffer the ignominy of having a United States Secretary of State telling them what to do. But Dean Rusk (U.S. Secretary of State when Barbados became independent in 1966) could not tell me what to do. Dean Rusk could not tell me to accept money from President (Lyndon) Johnson. I think President Johnson was the greatest of American Presidents.

But I will not accept any arms from President Johnson for myself or Barbados; and, therefore, we have no right to be joining this queue of mendicants.

We never had a cent from the United States government, and I am proud of it, and I do not think the Barbadians were worse off then, than they are today. Begging from the United States is not going to solve our economic problems.

No turning back

Address to the 30th Annual Conference of the Democratic Labour Party at the George Street Auditorium on 25 August, 1985

Officers and members of the Executive Council and General Council of this great 30-year-old mature political organisation,
Delegates to this Conference,
Members of our Party,
Specially invited guests, distinguished visitors and friends,

This morning, I addressed the conference, as I am required to do by our Constitution as President for the time being of the Democratic Labour Party, when I delivered the report from the General Council for the year's activities which we have just concluded. You also received reports from the General Secretary on the work of the Executive Council and from the Deputy Leader of the opposition on the performance of our parliamentary group. Financial reports duly concluded the purely domestic and internal organisational matters which concern you on these occasions.

This afternoon, after having satisfied our inward and physical hunger, we have been intellectually refreshed by contributions made by our tried and trusted friends and companions in our struggle for social justice and economic freedom in the Caribbean in the persons of Comrade Michael Norman Manley and Frank Leslie Walcott. By the rousing applause with which you responded to them, I am convinced that you will go on your separate journeys at the end of the day stimulated and inspired to greater efforts in the cause of solidarity of all our people, but primarily on behalf of the down trodden and the oppressed. I wish publicly to express my personal thanks to both and to admit my eternal indebtedness for their support.

I consider myself fortunate to be able to resolve what, at first blush, would appear to be a dichotomy in that I spoke to you earlier and now rise to speak again.

You listened to the President and Chairman of the General Council of this party this morning Sinn Fein and Apar Jal domestically and for us alone. For your ears only.

This afternoon, I am speaking as Political Leader and for all the world to hear. *Coram populo*. There is no secrecy over who we are; where we have come from; what we stand for or where we are going.

There are no latter day socialists or fifth angels amongst us. We are they who are coming out of great tribulation; out of systematic victimisation; out of economic deprivation; we are they who intend to remove fear and tremor from the hearts and minds of our young people by reasserting the sovereignty of our nation and by restoring the sense of dignity and self-respect which every Barbadian man and woman and every child at home and abroad felt and enjoyed before their economic and social freedoms were torn from them page by page, step by step by the collection of political opportunists and cynical bandits who have subverted the original aims and principles of an early labour organisation and are now masquerading under the title of its founders for their own personal gain and financial aggrandisement.

It has never been any part of our style either in our manifesto at election time, or on our public platforms to excoriate the other people for their misdeeds. We have been vocal on issues which adversely affect the general populace. Ours has never been a party for beating of the chest or indulging in campaigns of slander against our adversaries. We have leaned over backwards to present a positive image to the electorate and we have frequently repressed, in the national interest, matters which we felt would reflect adversely on all Barbadians if they should become publicly ventilated.

Not so the bandits. Parliamentary privilege has been used as a shelter to defame private persons who do not share the same perverted views of society as the political directorate and heap vulgar abuse on and impeach the professional integrity of members of the opposition despite appeals to the presiding officers for a return to decency and standards of rectitude.

The prostitution of the media has been facilitated by the flagrant abuse of power of withdrawal of work permits and to quote the present Prime Minister, speaking of the late Prime Minister, I quote, 'the law of libel was his friend'. In this atmosphere truth and justice can never sprout from under the damp cloggy soil of repression, far less flourish.

The highly qualified, well educated young people of the Constituency of Saint John,* have had to resort to the device of giving

*The constituency which Mr Barrow represented for nearly 3 years.

addresses of relatives living in other parts of the island when applying for jobs in the public service. To that degree, even have the public officers been subverted in this country. The society has become polarised to the extent that there are ominous rumblings beneath the surface. The front line is no longer only in Sharpesville and Notting Hill, the front line stretches from Belleville to My Lords Hill. At no time between 1948 and 1985 have the battle lines been more clearly drawn between the welfare of the people and the interests of the few. We were far on the road to achieving a level of understanding in this country where every man, woman and child felt that he or she counted for something; where he or she felt that here in this country existed possibilities for self-realisation and fulfilment; where mendicancy and dependence were not regarded as the inevitable fate of those persons who were not born to wealth and position.

Not so anymore. Survival is the main preoccupation of the masses. Otherwise respectable women find that they have to do favours in order to provide food for their children.

We have reverted to the bad old Vestry days where people lined up for fifty cents, but the largesse is doled out on afternoons in Tweedside Road instead of in the morning at Temple Gardens.

Unemployed and destitute persons are a threat in many ways to the stability of this or any society. A person with a job is a free person. A person without a job becomes cynical after a time and does not consider that he owes the society the responsible disposition of his voting power. That is why all of us must work primarily to eradicate the scourge of unemployment.

It is a matter of enlightened self interest. The former President of the International Bank for Reconstruction and Development, Mr Robert McNamara, once spoke of the unproductive poor who instead of contributing to the national output impoverished us all. Unemployed relatives and strangers not only fail to contribute by way of taxes to the national revenues but impoverish their relatives and friends by reducing their disposable incomes which they have to share with them.

It is, therefore, a matter of top priority that the Democratic Labour Party take urgent, effective measures to set the people to work again. We can take no political satisfaction that unemployment in this country under the present regime is at a dangerously high level.

Some of the measures which we propose have been set out in our Anniversary booklet.

There is a school of thought which supports the idea that we should not let the other people know what we propose to do. In this school, I have never enrolled. I am a Barbadian and my politics are not conspiratorial to be sprung on a surprised electorate only at election time. My policies are the same yesterday, tomorrow and for evermore. I do not believe in gimmicks. In human behaviour and economic inter-relationships, there are only so many scenarios. What is often lacking is the political will and ability to pursue the right remedies.

I have no hesitation in declaring what we will do because I know from experience that even after you have told them that, they don't know how to do it, just as they didn't know how we were going to introduce free secondary education right up the day before school opened in January 1962 and so insisted that it could not be done.

I must now turn to two matters which have been promoted to a level of national discussion recently in the press of this island. Those of you who have worked closely with me will know that I do not allow myself to be provoked into conducting debates on public or private issues in the columns of the press. My political and legal reputations, unlike some of my opponents, have never depended on the fabrications of the media, but rather on my direct performances in real terms. If the media do not make you, they cannot break you. Consequently, even well-meaning and honest journalists find it difficult to secure interviews or responses from me as they will all confirm, chiefly because even in public life, I am a private person. If my name never appears in the press, even if I won a prize of great value, I would remain completely unconcerned.

When I was serving in the Royal Air Force, the only thing the press had to say about me gleefully was that I had been killed in action three times.

But when the British News Services relayed the information that I was commissioned as a Pilot Officer in the field, your press couldn't take it, so they reported that it was someone else's son who had been so distinguished. They disavowed the Minister of the Gospel who has never disclaimed his paternity.

I was called to the Bar and earned my degree with neither the notice or assistance of any local or any other media. Since being in opposition, I have travelled to Australia where I was elected Vice President of the Westindies Players Association. I have travelled to Tanzania, Taiwan, Nigeria, Rome and San Francisco on business without any retinue paid for by the taxpayers. I have not been to Beijing or any country in the Eastern bloc because I had no clients or calling in any of those places. I hope that when I am called to my reckoning, since I do not require or need any outpouring of hypocrisy or glass-enclosed shrine, that they will omit to even mention my name except to demand, if anyone tries to place me outside the laws of Barbados, a Coroner's inquest with full disclosure of the reasons for my withdrawal from this mortal scene. My mortal remains, after incineration, may be scattered from an aircraft in the Caribbean Sea without any of the ghoulish and undignified caterwauling that passes for services in one of our main places of political public entertainment.

All of this is a personal explanation why I have not commented before today on the recently held conference on the Latin American and Caribbean Debt Problem which I attended in Havana between 30 July and the 3rd day of August this year.

This Conference was attended by over 1,200 persons from Latin America and the Caribbean, including a large number of ex-presidents of countries like Mexico, Venezuela, Dominican Republic, former Prime Ministers like Mr Michael Manley and myself, several Bishops of the Roman Catholic Church, Priests of the Anglican Churches, head of the Evangelical movement in Puerto Rico, capitalist owners of the conservative press in Latin America and others.

The reasons why governments were not active in the conference was because the governments were legally responsible for incurring the heavy debt burden and could not be expected to deal with the very serious implication in full and frank discussions.

In 1975 Michael Manley and I urged at the United Nations Organisation that a New International Economic Order should be promoted.

In his letter of invitation in 1985, the President of Cuba stated, 'the analysis of the debt must be linked to the promotion of the New International Economic Order adopted at the U.N. but ignored at the same time, despite the constant demands for global negotiations that the under-developed countries continue making'.

It is quite clear that the burden of the debt is so heavy that many countries in our hemisphere will never be able to repay the commercial banking system. The current debt owed by Latin American and Caribbean countries is of the magnitude of three hundred and sixty thousand million dollars, and the interest payments alone call for a transfer of 40 billion dollars annually from the underdeveloped countries to the private banking interests mainly of the United States of America. It is an oversimplification to suggest that the Havana conference was a conspiracy to repudiate the debts incurred by the Third World countries, although it is clear that many of them simply cannot pay.

President Castro himself clearly expressed the view that alternative solutions must be found and that there should be a dialogue between creditors and debtors.

Since I had personal views that may have distressed some of the delegates or the hosts of the meeting, I refrained from expressing my opinions before that pluralistic gathering but contented myself within the role of keeping order at the session at which I was invited to be Chairman.

Here in Barbados, I have to state unequivocally that each debtor country must decide the approach which will do the least damage to the respective economies.

In the first place, some of the debts should never have been incurred at all. Governments and bankers negotiated the debts. People and taxpayers from here to eternity are being called upon to pay. Many Latin American governments were sold, and sometimes bribed, by money lenders to incur debts, which although they may have fattened the pockets of the bankers and their lawyers, have done nothing to increase the productive capacities of the borrowing countries or to improve the general well-being of their citizens. Governments borrow. People repay. A case in point is the [Barbados] Central Bank building which, in order to imbue it with a spirit of righteousness, Her Majesty the Queen wil be invited to plaquate sometime in October. Many of the military regimes in Latin America and the Caribbean borrowed money for arms and militaristic purposes which could only be employed against their own people who are now being called upon to pay. Here in Barbados as well.

It is clearly not in the interest of this country to proclaim that all debts should be repudiated since we are both creditors and debtors. We are in dire need of the $130 million owed to us either by the Caribbean Multilateral Clearing Facility or the government of Guyana or by both.

When the Democratic Labour Party peacefully turned over the government in Spetember 1976, the total external debt of Barbados was $49.1 million and the National Debt was $258 million.

I have no intention of repudiating that debt because we have a hospital, Deep Water Harbour, many schools, the Caribbean Development Bank, our share of the U.W.I (University of the Westindies) capital cost, the East Coast Road, the Pine Hill Dairy and other physical productive assets to show for it.

Today the foreign indebtedness of every man, woman and child is $1,600 per capita with a foreign debt of $457 million and a total net debt of $1 billion and a debt service charge of $105 million out of revenue this year, as compared with $19 million in 1976.

A serious examination of the debt problem, therefore, is required before we are plunged into a depression more serious than that which afflicted us from 1929 onwards. There is no single simplistic solution. But I can say here and now that the friendly governments such as Canada and the international institutions who mainly assisted with worthwhile projects, have nothing to be apprehensive over the good sense of responsibility of the Democratic Labour Party.

The money sharks and influence brokers, however, who have shared out patronage on a vast scale while extorting exorbitant conditions, will have to bear the full scrutiny of public examination.

No wonder their sycophants are worried over the Havana Conference. The Democratic Labour Party is a free and independent organisation owing allegiance to no foreign country or local vested interest other than to the people of Barbados itself.

The next media debate concerned the entry of Mr Philip Goddard[**] into the political arena. This causes me neither surprise nor distress. This is a free democratic society and Phillip Goddard is free to associate himself with any group which he considers will best project his personal interests, political and social prejudices and family investments.

I wish to state, however, that despite rumours circulated by the Barbados Labour Party adherents, I have had no discussion with Phillip Goddard at any time in my life concerning his becoming a member or running as a candidate for the Democratic Labour Party. Neither have I authorised anyone to approach or speak to him with such an object in view.

Anyone who wishes to associate with the DLP with a view to seeking public office, must first

(a) apply for membership;
(b) demonstrate an interest in representing people in and out of election time;
(c) subscribe to our philosophy of Democratic Socialism;
(d) convince the Executive Council that they are not merely office seekers or opportunists but share our genuine concerns.

We do not pick our people up off the street.

By none of these critera has Philip Goddard qualified himself, but his candidature for the B.L.P. (Barbados Labour Party) has clearly defined the type of party they are,and the interest which they have all

[**] A member of a wealthy white Barbadian family

138

along represented.

Sometime within the next twelve months, the people of Barbados will be called upon to go to their polling stations to choose a government to manage the affairs of this country for a period of five years from the date of return of the writs.

That is what an election is about. There are two major political parties in this country and both of them have had the opportunity to demonstrate their ability, or lack of it, to manage the affairs of the country in which we live.

The record of the Democratic Labour Party is one of which we can justly be proud. The record of the other people is one of which I am, as a Barbadian, deeply ashamed. In their time, we have witnessed sharp increases in crimes of violence, drug peddling, interference with the due process of law, over taxation, rising unemployment, and all the ills that flesh can be heir to; depite our woes, there has been on the part of our political masters a truculent vaingloriousness, a disregard for all standards of ethical behaviour, and a lowering of the morale of civil establishment, while boosting the militaristic ambitions of the uniformed militia.

The invasion of privacy, unlawful detentions, cover-up of white collar crime – these have all been on the increase.

Democratic elections require a purification of the electoral process. The appointment of the electoral boundaries commission will not in itself guarantee that the electoral lists will not be perverted by unscrupulous enumerators. Already we have had to protest the conduct of some of these persons and removal and substitution have sometimes been effected.

In the last analysis, victory can be ensured only by the high quality and dedication of our candidates. I need to be convinced that people who offer themselves as candidates understand the nature of the battle we face and are determined to put a maximum effort to ensure a victory for the Democratic Labour Party.

We have no space on board this shuttle for people who are looking for social status or economic benefit. The money is on the other side. The sacrifices are on our side. No candidate for the D.L.P. is to consider he is taking a shot at being an M.P. (Member of Parliament), like it is some kind of 'Lucky Dip' or 'Let's Go to the Races Sweep'. We shall have to evaluate our performances day by day and week by week. Those who are weary, those who are languid, should go to the Lord and be at rest. There will be no rest for the valiant. No turning back; no time for self-doubt. No time for self-pity. No time for mistakes.

Mistakes can be detected.
Mistakes can be corrected.
But I'm asking you – for heaven's sake –
Please don't make the same mistakes.

A robust Errol Walton Barrow (left) rises to address the Democratic Labour Party's 1985 convention to a standing ovation from the floor as well as from the invited guest – Jamaica's opposition People's National Party (PNP) leader, Michael Manley, and Barbados Workers' Union (BWU) General Secretary, Frank L, Walcott.

 Less than a year later, in May 1986, Mr Barrow led the DLP to a massive victory at the Polls, and named Mr Walcott President of the upper house of the Barbados Parliament, the Senate.

141

Errol Walton Barrow stokes the coals at a beach barbecue in the seaside resort of Bath in the constituency he served for nearly 30 years – the Parish of St. John on Barbados's rugged Atlantic-washed eastern coast.

The beach picnic marked the Democratic Labour Party's 25th anniversary celebrations.

Errol Walton Barrow (third from the right) presides over a session of a Western-Hemisphere wide conference on the Third World debt held in Havana, Cuba in the summer of 1985.

Mr Barrow, then leader of the opposition in Barbados, is flanked by Jamaican opposition leader, Mr Michael Manley (on his right), and Cuban President, Fidel Castro (on his left).

At extreme right, is Cuban Vice President, Carlos Rafael Rodriguez.

"What kind of image do you have of yourself?"

Address to a political rally 13 May, 1986, at which the Democratic Labour Party's 27 candidates for the general elections of 28 May, 1986 were introduced

What I wish to speak to you about very briefly here this evening is about you. About yourself.

I want to know what kind of mirror image do you have of yourself? That is what I am concerned about. What kind of mirror image do you have of yourself? Do you really like yourselves? Because you can never really like anybody unless you first like yourself. There are too many people in Barbados who despise themselves and their dislike of themselves reflects itself in their dislike of other people...people who live next door to them, members of their family, husbands, and wives, and the ox and the ass and the stranger within the gates.

I would like to say that in 1951, 1956, 1961 the Conservatives used to do a few favours for people.

A planter would send a man who had a little influence, let us say in Ellerton Village in St. George, send him down to Plantations Limited or Manning and Company and get some lumber to repair the old house, or if he had a cheap canvasser you would send him to Detco Motors and let him trust a new car. And those people would be motivated into giving their support to the Conservative candidate because of the favours which used to be given out to them.

But it really did not matter because the people who accepted that kind of help thought that they would be beholden to the rich people of this island, because the rich people were in a position to do personal favours for them. But what the rich people in Barbados did not realise is that they did not have money to do favours for everybody who had the right to vote after universal adult suffrage.

That was all right when you had 250 people voting in St. Thomas, and probably 178 voting in St. Andrew, and probably 311 voters in St. Lucy, but when you have 38,000 voting alone in St. Michael – voting

144

for two candidates, not even John D. Rockefeller himself would be able to do enough favours for 38,000 people to persuade them to go and cast their votes and exercise their suffrage against the Labour Party's interest, in favour of that wealthy person.

Which group is wealthiest in Barbados then? Who has the most money to spend? There has never been anybody in the history of Barbados with six million dollars at his disposal. The Tom Adams government had $600 million in each and every year at its disposal to bribe you with your own money, and then spit in your face.

So the Conservatives now can save their money. They are not going to France and Italy anymore because of terrorism, but they are going to Tampa, Florida, Vancouver, British Columbia and California, because they have people now who will spend the workers' money to bribe the workers and they could save their money and thus go off and live like true politicians, while they use your money against you.

Now what has bothered me in this society is that every time after elections, people expect certain things to take place. And although the law says that he that giveth is as much guilty of bribery and corruption under the Corrupt Practices Act as he that receiveth, we know that even on the polling day, people are given envelopes with $100 bills in them.

Philip Greaves[*] and Asquith Phillips[*] and I sat down trying to get people to bring affidavits, so that we could lock up some of them. Our own people, registered Democratic Labour Party people, said they were not prepared to go into court and swear.

So what kind of mirror image would you have of yourself? If there are corrupt ministers in Barbados tonight, you have made them corrupt.

I am not trying to make any excuses for you, but I realise what has happened in this society. You have people who are living on the brink of, and at, subsistence level. I look around and see people who have not done an honest day's work in their whole lives driving around in MP[**]cars, having an ostentatious standard of living, unlike my poor families in St. John, who the Welfare Officer gives $50 to feed a family of ten for a whole week.

What kind of mirror image can you have of yourself?

[*](Philip Greaves is an attorney-at-law and is now Deputy Prime Minister. Mr Greaves, Mr Asquith Philips and Mr Barrow worked out of the same chambers in the 1976-86 period during which Mr Barrow's Democratic Labour Party was out of office.)

[**](MP is the prefix on the licence plates of Government registered motor vehicles).

Let me tell you what I mean by 'image you have of yourself'. You so much despair of this society that you queue up at Trident House (United States Consulate) day after day. Those of you who have read Julius Caesar would know the passage that says: 'You have sat the live long day with patient expectation to see great Pompey pass the streets of Rome.' And you have stood the live long day with patient expectation for the man to tell you down there that you can't get the visa to get on the 400 to New York next week.

Your greatest ambition is to try to prove to the people of the United States Consulate that you are only going up to visit your family, when you know very well that when you get up there, you los' 'way. And you are surprised when the people at the United States Embassy tell you that you do not have a strong reason to return to Barbados. And you are the only person dishonest enough with yourself to realise that you do not have a strong reason to return to Barbados, because Barbados has nothing to offer you. You are not being honest with yourself, but you tell the man down there, 'Oh yes, I'm returning.'

If I had to answer that question now I would be in trouble, because under this dispensation for the past ten years, I never had a strong reason to come back here.

But I want to tell you this, that I believe that I am as much Barbadian as they are and I do not like my country being run down the way it has been run down since 1976, and that is the reason why I return.

When I went to Mexico, I had to make a decision, and I returned; I went to the Pacific and I had to make a decision and I returned. I had a strong reason. My reason is that I did not want to see my country go down the drain but you who are not in politics, don't have a strong reason. Tell me one good strong reason you have to return to Barbados.

Your mirror image of yourself is that your ambition in life is to try and get away from this country. And we could call ourselves an independent nation? When all we want do is to go and scrub somebody's floors and run somebody's elevator or work in some-body's store or drive somebody's taxi in a country where you catching your royal when the winter sets in?

What kind of mirror image do you have of yourself? Let me tell you what kind of mirror image I have of you, or what the Democratic Labour Party has of you. The Democratic Labour Party has an image that the people of Barbados would be able to run their own affairs, to pay for the cost of running their own country, to have an education system which is as good as what can be obtained in any industrialised country, anywhere in the world.

It is only now that you are reading that in the state of Texas, the government of the state has asked to make the teachers pass an examination – you know what kind of examination? To see if they can read and write!

The gentleman of the Texas teachers' union came on the news and he said that he was very proud of the result because only eight per cent of the teachers couldn't read and write!

If (President Ronald) Reagan had to take the test, I wonder if he would pass. But this is the man that you all say in the newspapers, how great he is for bombing the people in Libya and killing little children. I am no (Libyan leader Mu'ammar) Qathafi supporter. I don't know Qathafi and I have never had any desire to go to Libya. But this is the man that you all go up to at the airport and put down a red carpet for, and he is the President of a country in which in one of the more advanced and biggest states eight per cent of the teachers cannot read and write, and he feels that they are better than we. And you feel that we should run up there and bow.

What kind of mirror image do you have of yourself? Why don't you sit down there and start trying to put people on the moon, too? Instead of using $100 million to develop the potential of the young scientists that we have, and the young doctors that we have, we spend it putting up an expression of a momumental edifice behind the Cathedral and call it a Central Bank Building, because we think that people develop by ostentation, by showing off, and not by developing people.

But when a government steals from people in the way of consumption taxes and takes that money and spends it on their own high lifestyles, and unnecessary buildings, then that government not only has contempt for you, but what is most unfortunate, you have contempt for yourself, because you allow them to do it.

And you get the Prime Minister of the country saying that his ambition is to have the same kind of lifestyle as the people in the United States enjoy. I wonder what kind of lifestyle he is enjoying now? And then his successor goes outside of Barbados and says we are drifting away in Barbados from the Westminster model of parliamentary democracy, and we are easing into a presidential system; that we want a presidential system, so that, like Reagan, they can go and bomb. They can go and bomb the mental people in the hospital in Grenada and the little children in Benghazi, in Tripoli? Is that what we want a presidential system for?

We don't have a Presidential system yet. But you have people who are employed and paid with your taxes who could buy a boat and give it to an Englishman to smuggle arms into Barbados. I can give you the name and the place and everything you want.

We don't have a presidential system, but you can have people removing money from a Canadian Imperial Bank account and people who are in charge of the institutions in this island, and transferring it to the Barbados National Bank without the authority of the people from whose account the money was being withdrawn. I know it is so, because I told (Prime Minister Bernard) St John who it was and that man has not been locked up yet.

I told him then that you should never appoint a person to a responsible statutory corporation in this island who is accustomed to forging people's signatures. And then he went outside and came back and never said a word. And you allow that to go on in Barbados.

And there are poeple in high places in this island who conspired to allow that to happen, because the gentlemen was fined $1,000 for so doing, and not by the law courts, but by a private group of people who got together and said, 'You committed forgery; we are going to fine you $1,000.' So you circumvent the Director of Public Prosecutions, and you hold your own dumb-head court martial and then you present him with a big bowl and congratulate him on his achievements.

What kind of an image do you have of yourself if you allow this kind of thing to happen?

What kind of an image do you have of yourself when you allow the mothers of this nation to be beasts of burden in the sugarcane fields? In Mexico where people suffer under a lower standard of living than in Barbados, they use donkeys to freight canes out of the fields.

In Antigua, they use a small railway; but here the mothers of the nation with sons at Harrison College, the Alleyne School and daughters at Queen's College, St Michael and Alexandra – they are used as beasts of burden and there is no shelter in any of those sugar cane fields. I have talked time and time again to the Barbados Workers' Union about this and you allow that to continue. What kind of image do you have of yourself?

I suggested, and I was inspired by the work done by the late Mr Ernest Bevin, who was (British) Foreign Minister, who went to work at eight – I don't mean 8 o' clock in the morning, I mean eight years of age – and those dock workers in London used to turn up during the winter and summer from 5 o'clock in the morning waiting for a ship, and if a ship didn't come in for three weeks or three months, they wouldn't get any pay. And Ernest Bevin introduced the guaranteed week for dock workers. I set up a commission of enquiry into the sugar industry and made the examination of the guaranteed week for agricultural workers one of the terms of reference of that commission, and the commission reported that nobody gave any evidence before them in support of this recommendation.

What kind of mirror image do the people of the Workers' Union, of whom we have members, have, even of you or themselves? And I had to wait until there was a dispute in the sugar industry and we had television and get on a blackboard and say, well these will be the wages from next week and on Tuesday I went into the House (of Assembly) and introduced the guaranteed wages for agricultural workers.

Why should only one man have a mirror image of you that you do not want to have of yourself? What kind of society are we striving for? There is no point in striving for Utopia, but you do not realise your potential.

You have heard the opportunities which our members have taken to improve themselves by going to certain institutions and so on – not that we believe that people with good education are the only people who can be in politics. The very fact that a man has made the effort and taken the time to improve himself shows that he has the kind of calibre which would make him a useful representative of the people.

I lived in a little country when I was young, the Virgin Islands. It was just bought from Denmark by the United States of America. My father was a Chancellor. I was too young to go when he was transferred. So when I was three months old, I went.

There is no unemployment in that country. They don't manage their affairs as well as we did in the past. They don't receive any big lot of grants and loans and that kind of thing, even from the United States.

They have to bring in workers. They have the largest oil refinery in the western hemisphere run by a man called Hess. But that is a small country. But there is another small country which is run by a friend of mine. The country has 210 square miles; it is 40 square miles bigger than Barbados. If you took the Parish of St Phillip and put it right in the little curve by Bathsheba that would be the size of the country of Singapore of Lee Kwan Yew.

But you know the difference between Barbados and that country? First, Barabdos has 250,000 people. You know how many people Singapore has on 40 more square miles? Over two-and-a-half million, on an island just a little larger than Barbados.

They don't have any sugar plantations; they don't have enough land to plant more than a few orchids on. It is one of the orchid centres of the world. They grow orchids in Singapore. They don't have enough land to plant a breadfruit tree in the backyard and nearly every Barbadian, even in the metropolitan area of Bridgetown, would have some kind of fruit tree in the backyard.

Sixty per cent of those three million persons have been housed by the government of Singapore. They don't have any oil for ministers to steal. They don't have any beaches like we have here. There are people here in this audience, Barbadians who have served in Singapore, who can tell you about Singapore. There is no unemployment in Singapore.

They have developed an education system but they are teaching people things that are relevant to the 21st century. They are not teaching people how to weed by the road. They are in the advance of the information age.

But you know the difference between you and them? They have got a mirror image of themselves. They are not looking to get on any plane to go to San Francisco. Too far away. The government does not encourage them to emigrate unless they are going to develop business for Singapore.

They have a mirror image of themselves. They have self-respect. They have a desire to move their country forward by their own devices. They are not waiting for anybody to come and give them handouts. And there is no unemployment.

Is that the mirror image that you have of yourself? Anyhow, ladies and gentleman, I done.

Errol Barrow asks: "What Kind of Mirror Image Do You Have of Yourself?" at a political rally just prior to the May 28, 1986 general elections.

The rally in Independence Square, Bridgetown, was used to introduce the DLP's 27 candidates for the elections.

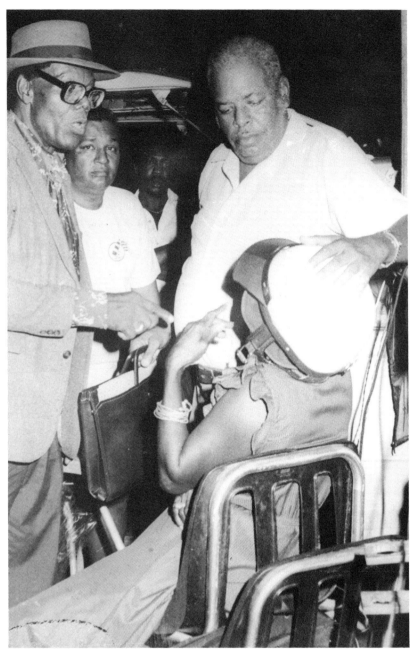

*A consoling hand from Errol Barrow during a visit with ordinary Barbadians.
At left (wearing hat) is Mr Clarence "Coloured" Ward, a faithful supporter of the
Democratic Labour Party throughout its existence.*

Errol Barrow on the campaign trail during the run-up to the 1986 general elections in which his Democratic Labour Party (DLP) won an overwhelming 24 out of the 27 seats in the Barbados House of Assembly.

Above, Mr Barrow is moved to show an enthusiastic crowd of thousands some fancy footwork during an "Evening with the Dems" at Queens Park near Bridgetown.

Mr Barrow (standing) and supporters show off the brooms with which they intended to sweep the then ruling Barbados Labour Party out of office.

Errol Walton Barrow absorbing the adulation from a crowd of thousands of supporters in Bridgetown on the eve of the 1986 general elections.

Errol Barrow (third from left) smiles an acknowledgement of congratulations from party supporters after the 1986 general election victory of his Democratic Labour Party (DLP).
This was one of a series of stops for a number of island-wide motorcades that marked the victory, and the end of ten years of BLP rule in Barbados.

Errol Walton Barrow's hour of victory – 25 years apart!
Surrounded by friends, and mobbed by supporters, Premier-designate Barrow (in cap and dark glasses) raises his hand in a victory salute after the December 1961
general elections which his Democratic Labour Party (DLP) won for the first time.

A considerably more restrained Errol Barrow is seen being interviewed by Barbados television moments after he led his DLP to an overwhelming victory in the May 1986 general elections.

Caribbean Integration:
The reality and the goal

Address to the Caribbean Community Heads of
Governments Conference, 3 July 1986,
Georgetown, Guyana

Mr Secretary General,
Mr President,
Your Excellencies,
Distinguished Colleagues,
Fellow Prime Ministers,
Ladies and Gentlemen,

> "The Street is in darkness,
> Children are sleeping,
> Mankind is dreaming,
> It is midnight.
>
> "Who will awaken
> One little flower
> Sleeping and growing
> Hour and hour?
>
> "Light will awaken
> All the young flowers
> Sleeping and growing
> Hour and hour.
>
> "Dew is awake
> Morning is soon
> Mankind is risen
> Flowers will bloom."

The celebrated national poet of Guyana, Martin Carter, in his poem
'For My Son' reminds us in these moving stanzas that we represent

the expectations of five million human beings, and what is more that what we achieve or betray concerns not only the living, but those who are not yet born.

There are many critical questions on our agenda. There will be many different, even conflicting views. We have a long experience in surviving such differences. And we will survive them again. But there is a fundamental theme on which I should like to think there can be no difference. And that is the absolute necessity to promote and defend the solidarity and the sovereignty of this regional Caribbean family, and also the absolute obligation to discover those strategies and mechanisms which will ultimately lead to unity of action in all major areas of our economic, social and political life. If we have sometimes failed to comprehend the essence of the regional integration movement, the truth is that thousands of ordinary Caribbean people do, in fact, live that reality every day. In Barbados, our families are no longer exclusively Barbadian by island origin. We have Barbadian children of Jamaican mothers; Barbadian children of Antiguan and St Lucian fathers. And there is no need to mention Trinidad and Tobago which has always been tied to us not only by the inestimable bonds of consanguinity, but by the burgeoning cross fertilisation of cultural art forms. We are a family of islands nestling closely under the shelter of the great Co-operative Republic of Guyana. And this fact of regional togetherness is lived every day by ordinary Westindian men and women in their comings and goings.

The small traders, and some not so small, who move from Jamaica to Haiti on what I believe, is their legitimate business. The same with Grenada and Trinidad, Barbados and St Lucia and Dominica. What some people call the underground economy. It is true that the laws of each territory may sometimes get in their way, but for the majority of these decent and industrious sons and daughters of the Caribbean, I believe their business is spontaneous though unassisted, and legitimate though unregulated. I should like to believe that we are all committed to the principle of mobility and people interaction. To the principle, I repeat. And that we have an obligation to think and go on thinking out ways how such a principle might be applied without imposing on any territory a greater strain than its resources are able to support.

The point I want to emphasise is this: the regional integration movement is a fact of daily experience. It is a reality which is lived, but which we have not yet been able to institutionalise. What is the source of our failure? I should like to share some of my own misgivings. The first has to do with communication and the ways in which we communicate. For many of our people, the regional integration movement has come to mean matters which relate exclusively to trade. Who will buy my shirts and on what conditions? Whose markets will open up for my pepper sauce, my guava jelly, who will buy my white sand, who will buy my grey sand? These are realistic questions; but we have made them the exclusive justification for our being together. And this has been a grave shortcoming. Whether we recognise it or not, we have a cultural history, a common experience of feeling which goes deeper and is much older than CARICOM and the negotiations about trade.

My attention was drawn recently to an essay by the Jamaican artist and scholar, Rex Nettleford, who articulates what I am trying to say about the essence of the regional movement which transcends mere discussions on trade. Jamaica is the occasion, but it is the Caribbean he is addressing. I quote:

> "The public opinion polls can tell you what are the feelings of a day or moment; they cannot tell you what are the deeper social and psychological needs of our people who have had to devise strategies and stratagems of survival against the ravages of severance and suffering, and the continuing deprivation in economical, social and political terms ... Such strategies are the result and clear sign of a collective intellect, a collective wisdom that resides among our ordinary folk. But that collective wisdom continues to be ignored on account of the arrogance of planners trained in the North Atlantic or even at the University of the Westindies, especially when the UWI forgets that it is not an extension of Oxbridge. The collective wisdom and intellect of our people are yet to be tapped and given central place in the development strategy of our nation. But we are so busy Westminsterising ourselves into becoming a clone of the Anglo-Saxon world and its American extension that we forget that we have a life and history of our own to be examined, dealt with and used as a source of energy for the development of this nation/region and the shaping of a civilised society."

In every territory of our Caribbean region – and it has been my own experience in Barbados – I believe we have been failing to find a way of using the 'collective wisdom' of our people. We have not been able to communicate the essence and the cultural infrastructure of the regional integration movement. We have not been able to get people's minds to move beyond the constraints of trade. As a result, the slightest discord between two Prime Ministers over some restrictions affecting a type or quantity of wearing apparel can plunge citizens of the two countries into verbal and electronic warfare. The promise of the regional integration movement, even in the area of trade, cannot be realised unless we find new ways of communicating to the mass of our people the meaning and purpose of all our regional institutions. And that's one reason (if no other could be found) why the University must move from the confines of the campus more and more into the heart of the communities which constitute our region. This battle of communication in defence of the unity of the region, must be won if our efforts during this week and hitherto are to survive beyond the confines of conferences. Every institution and organisation should feel the obligation to accept this challenge: the national and regional media; the schools at all levels of instruction;the Church, every gathering that goes by the name of Caribbean should feel this obligation to accept this challenge of communication; to propogate the message that the region is a larger concept than trade, and that the future of trade arrangements may be favourably influenced by that conviction among the mass of ordinary people whose 'collective wisdom' I believe, with Nettleford, is a fact and very much alive.

The University of the Westindies has provided us over more than one generation with some very remarkable social scientists. I recall with a certain pride the excellent work which was done by the New World Group over the 1960s. Every major sector of our economic life has come under their scrutiny: Sugar, Bauxite, Oil, Tourism. Girvan and Thomas and Carrington, Brewster and Beckford, and, of course, Lloyd Best; Investigation which has always concerned the Institute of Social and Economic Research whose former Director, Allister McIntyre, is with us today. They proved beyond any doubt that this region is not lacking in intellectual human resources. But in spite of all this excellent work, an important link was missing. All this analysis, all this valuable organisation of information never got very far beyond the small circle of specialists for and by whom it was written. There was no link between that great storehouse of knowledge and the toiling mass of workers who are the motor force of any society. The analysis may be brilliant, the recommendations very ingenious; but these will serve a very limited purpose if their content does not become an essential part of the consciousness of the working population. This has been the curse of our societies: that division between those who work exclusively with their brains and those who, we think, work only with their hands. The truth is all men and women, irrespective of occupation, have to work with their brains. But this division of labour has made us most vulnerable where we needed to be most resilient. I am speaking of food and food production. We are worse than vulnerable. It is as though we had chosen to betray the blessings which God and nature has bestowed upon us. Surrounded by the richest of seas, we condemned ourselves to importing fish. Our lands can provide almost every known food crop, yet we persist in the luxury of imported vegetables.

I should like to recall a voice and a great mentor who was never without ideas about this danger and who tried to reverse this suicidal tendency which pervaded all our history. Dr Eric Williams will have to be heard again and again, whenever we say agriculture. He had a conception of food production which was regional. I quote him on the Caribbean Food Crisis:

> 'Food production must be approached as a basic industry to be run on commercial lines by a corporation collectively owned by the governments of the area and making approved investments in the different territories. This in practical terms, means a Caribbean Community Market ... I remind you that, last year, 1973, the Caribbean Community countries imported 24 million dollars worth of fertiliser of which only two million (or 10 per cent) came from Trinidad and Tobago ... Production must aim to satisfy not only the food needs of the local population of the Caribbean. It must also take into account the needs of the extensive tourist trade in such countries as Barbados and Jamaica, as well as the export market beginning with the Caribbean region: Suriname, the Netherlands Antilles, Haiti, the Dominican Republic ... and the commercial co-operation I envisage for the production of food on a large scale must keep the needs of those Caribbean areas in mind...'

Dr Eric Williams wanted to correct the preference for imported foods which has been a major cause of our psychological dependency before and after independence. And he wanted to help make agriculture a respected occupation because we needed it to make food production a respected industry because we cannot survive without it and because it also required gifts of intellect and high technical competence. He wanted to help put an end to the insult he heard school children exchanging about their past. I quote:

> 'I myself encountered .. a group of young people to whom I was speaking and who assured me they wish to have no part of any agricultural programme related to the small farmer and local foodstuff because commodities like eddoes and dasheen were slave food.'

The Colonel from the Confederate South has won the battle for the minds of our children. I'm happy to say I don't think this would happen in Dominica where school children are making agricultural work a normal part of their curriculum. And it is here we need to begin (in the schools) if we are going to correct this hostility directed towards the production of the food which is the very fuel of our existence; and if we are going to help another generation to understand why self-sufficiency may be one of the greatest forces of resistance to any form of external penetration.

But no amount of analysis, however brilliant, can save us from this danger without an informed and highly technical work-force in agricuture and the industries it generates.

My position also remains clear that the Caribbean must be recognised and respected as a zone of peace. In this connection, I should like to make further references to Eric Williams by saying that his speech, From Slavery to Chaguaramas, made in 1960 over the issue of the United States base, should be required reading in every school of the Caribbean and in every language of the Caribbean. Europe, and by extension the United States, have always thought it a perfectly natural duty to invade and occupy these territories. Columbus did not dicover the new world. He invaded it. Goerge Beckford asks the question, 'How can you discover somewhere, where people are already living?' We started our history as naval and military bases; that is, in our association with the modern world, each territory was there for capturing and recapturing. Eric Williams had this factor uppermost in mind in his argument over Chaguaramas; and he always argued from history. I quote him to emphasise why this document is so important today. He said:

> 'And as Europe went out, the U.S.A. came in. After getting their independence, which had been based on large scale trade connections with the Westindies, most of them illegal, most of them involving smuggling, the new U.S.A. began from the very start to look upon the Westindies and the Caribbean Sea as their sphere of influence.'

They began shortly after independence by publishing the Monroe Doctrine, stating that they would not want to see any extension of European colonialism in the Westindies. The ambition clearly stated in those days was to dominate the entire hemisphere.

But if the whole Westindian movement is towards control of its own affairs, I, too, should like to know the clause in Adam's will which denies the Westindian people a share of this world, especially a share of the world that rightly belongs to them.

Puerto Rico has become a launching pad for neo-colonisation of the region. We have also seen it used as a base for a number of military exercises whose purpose is clear. There have been joint manoeuvres of very great magnitude, Ocean Venture '81 and '82. A high ranking officer, in fact, the highest ranking U.S. officer of the U.S. Navy in Puerto Rico, based at Roosevelt Roads, explained their purpose when he said: 'the orchestra practised before playing in public'.

I have said, and I repeat that while I am Prime Minister of Barbados, our territory will not be used to intimidate any of our neighbours: be that neighbour Cuba or the U.S.A.

And I do not believe that size is necessarily the only criterion for determining these matters. But it is important to let people know where you stand if they will support you in what is a moral commitment to peace in our region.

So I return to Eric Williams and the great speech From Slavery to Chaguaramas:

> 'The enemy is not the submarine, or not the weapons which would be changed in 10 years and then changed in a 100 years after that ... the enemy is poverty, the enemy is the suppression of the talents of our population...'

Recently, I have been reading William Demas' very stimulating address to the Institute of International Affairs at the UWI, St Augustine; and I recommend it for serious study. But my attention particularly caught a quotation from the British economist, John Maynard Keynes, on the importance and power of ideas:

> 'Indeed, the world is ruled by little else. Practical men who believe themselves to be quite exempt from intellectual influence, are usually the slaves of some defunct economist ... Soon or late, it is ideas, not vested interests, which are for good or evil.'

And that's why I believe in encouraging young people to acquaint themselves with the great variety of prevailing ideas; for it is only through knowledge and critical acquaintance that they will be able to discriminate which ideas are relevant or subversive to their interests.

And the university must never be restricted, impeded, or harassed for fulfilling its intellectual function of introducing its students, critically and honestly to the great body of ideas which constitute the storehouse of human knowledge. The government of Barbados, of whose Cabinet I have the honour to be Chairman, will never circumscribe the University by demanding that the members of its staff should subscribe to some form of conventional wisdom or be uncritical of the government itself.

The Englishman, Keynes, recalled the importance of ideas. And in our own sea, the great Caribbean poet of the nineteenth century, Jose Marti, spoke of the relation of truth to dreams.

> 'A true man does not seek the path where advantage lies, but rather the path where duty lies; and that is the only practical man, whose dream of Today will be the Law of Tomorrow; because he knows that without a single exception, the Future lies on the side of Duty.'

I wish to add my personal welcome to you, Mr President, on your assumption of the mantle of leadership of your country, following the untimely passing of our colleague Forbes Burnham. I know that you share the vision which inspired the founding fathers of our integration movement, and which has served to sustain our Community in its moments of gravest difficulty. I wish you every success in your tenure both as Chairman of this Conference, and, as President of the Co-operative Republic of Guyana.

I take this opportunity also to commend our out-going Secretary-General for the sterling contribution he has made to CARICOM throughout his mandate. I wish him well in his future endeavours.

On behalf of the government of Barbados, I take this opportunity to acknowledge publicly all the warm messages of congratulations and good wishes I have received from my Caribbean colleagues both in Bridgetown and here in Georgetown.

Such expressions of goodwill have strengthened the commitment of my government to the principal foreign policy objective which it has set itself, namely: to strengthen the structure of the Caribbean Community by promoting mutual understanding among its members for the benefit of all peoples.

Mr President, Your Excellencies, Ministers, Distinguished Guests, Ladies and Gentlemen, permit me to conclude on a personal note by thanking you for your patience and to borrow from John Bunyan the words spoken by Mr Valiant for Truth in Pilgrim's Progress:

> 'Though with much difficulty I have come hither, yet I do not repent me of the trouble I have taken.'

Two of the English-speaking Caribbean's leading political thinkers – Errol Walton Barrow of Barbados (left), and Dr Eric Williams, Prime Minister of Trinidad and Tobago (right).

Their deaths have created a major vacuum in the political life of the entire region, which is yet to be filled.

'Caribbeanising' our legal system

Address to the graduating class of the Sir Hugh Wooding Law School of the University of the Westindies (UWI), St. Augustine, Trinidad 23 September, 1986.

Mr Chairman,
Lord Chief Justice,
My Lords, Your Excellencies,
Distinguished guests,
Members of the graduating class of the
Hugh Wooding Law School – 1986,
Ladies and gentlemen,

Lawyers are not supposed to speak without briefs and since I have no brief, I will be brief. It gives great pleasure in having been invited to address the graduates on this occasion. It must indeed be a happy occasion for all of you and for your families and friends assembled here who, during your period of study at Cave Hill and at St. Augustine, have given both moral and tangible support during a period of what you yourselves may have regarded as an odd year of fire, but you can now look back justifiably upon this experience as most worthwhile and a giant leap forward into the future.

Most people who enter the legal profession have done so because they consider being a lawyer as a congenial and socially acceptable means of earning a living. At times like these we have, from our benchers and guest speakers, a recital of high ideas to be aspired to, which even the Archangel Gabriel himself could not perform. I do not consider that lawyers are necessarily more ethical or have higher standards than any other honourable profession or vocation, and for that reason, I think that I can discard all the lofty sentiments about what lawyers should do and what lawyers should be and say to you that the essence of the performance of your duty should be based on humility, that, to be successful in this as in any other profession one has to like what one is doing and what is more important, particularly in law and to some extent medicine, you must know what you are doing. And in order to achieve these two objectives, a lawyer has to remain a student all the days of our lives. Legal training is essential to the development of our societies. It must be relevant. It must create an understanding of our constitutional and social histories. I hope that what I have to say now is not taken as a criticism of the practitioners here in the Caribbean, but I should like to give you an idea of the genesis of the Faculty of Law in the University of the Westindies and the two Law Schools which are so necessary a part of our legal training.

Some time in the late '60s, the authorities in the United Kingdom became somewhat concerned over the graduation of large numbers of persons from the Commonwealth, and they discovered or they claimed to have discovered, again due to their own fault, (their own fault in the sense that when we went as students to the United Kingdon, they claimed that we all looked alike) that some students were getting examinations taken for them by substitutes.

The system of legal education was very, very deficient. There was no contact between the lecturers and their students. The students could turn up periodically at examination time without having attended any lectures at all, and strange enough some of them passed. But in the early days, most of the persons who went to the four Inns of Court to become barristers were either the brilliant recipients of scholarships from their governments or graduates from one of the great universities in the United Kingdom. I do not have to call any names, such persons as Sir Hugh Wooding, Sir Lennox O'Reilly, Mr Norman Manley – you can name them. There was no danger at that time. But when the winds of change began to blow, and people flocked to the United Kingdon to seek job opportunities, many of them quite rightly felt that they should try to improve themselves and many enrolled at the Inns of Court. But many of them tried to work and to study at the same time, and anyone who has had a sojourn in that foggy climate (I'll try not to be pejorative) will understand that, whereas we have had great success stories in the United States of people, who by the sweat of their brow were able to pursue some courses of study and become successful professional persons, it was virtually impossible to do so in England. And due to the ingenuity of some of our compatriots in the Commonwealth from Far Eastern countries, some legally qualified persons who were reluctant to return to their own countries because of the turmoil which was going on at that time, and possibly for other personal reasons, decided that they would indulge in the profession of examination sitters. And under this scheme, any London Transport worker who had to work too hard by day and could not study by night, or some scion of a rich parent who never had the ability at all, could go to one of these examinees and for the payment of a small fee, get someone to take the exams for them. Now I want to make it abundantly clear – I am not aware anywhere in Trinidad and Tobago that there are such persons masquerading as lawyers. I wish I could say the same thing for Barbados because from the performances and the irrelevancies that I have witnessed during the past twenty years, I am not sure, I will not put it higher than that, that some of them were not the beneficiaries of the people whom I call practising examinees. But the Benchers at the Inns of Court became very concerned and urged upon us and upon what was then the Colonial Office that something should be done to rid them of these nuisances (to use the words of King Henry) – these turbulent nuisances, and encourage the establishment of the Law Faculties and these professional schools not only here in the Caribbean, but in Africa and the Far East as well.

We have been the beneficiaries of these malpractices. I say that because, from my experience, it would not be possible for anyone to attend the Hugh Wooding Law School or the Norman Manley Law School – we are such a small, close compact society – without his name, his abilities, and his physiognomy being well known to his tutors and to his fellow students. That is one reason and we can be certain that all the graduates who came on this platform here this evening are persons who rightfully deserve to be given the certificates which they have gained. So that the general public in Trinidad and Tobago and the Eastern Caribbean can be assured that our graduates are people who have faced the starter and completed the course and breasted the tape.

But there is another reason why the establishment of these facilities here in the Caribbean has been beneficial to the societies which they serve and it is this – that I personally found, even after practising in the Middle Temple although I am a Lincoln's Inn man, in London and coming back here, that the situations which I had to face as a young barrister or advocate were entirely different from those which prevailed in the United Kingdom.

I knew a fair amount of constitutional law, I like to think so, but I certainly did not know much about the constitutions of the Caribbean territories because it was no part of our curriculum. The law relating to Real Property here and Conveyancing was based on a system which had been introduced in the United Kingdom in 1925 – the great law reforms, when we were labouring in Barbados under the antiquated system predating 1868. So I had to start learning Real Property and Conveyancing all over again as a practitioner. And in many other respects I found that what we had had to study in the United Kingdom, while being of considerable advantage to practice in that country, these subjects were totally irrelevant. The only concession that I can remember that was made to the benighted colonies by the authorities at the Council of Legal Education was that they taught Roman-Dutch law as an optional subject for those persons who came from Guyana and Ceylon and countries who had had a history of Dutch occupation. And I am assured by my colleagues, such as the late Forbes Burnham, and later on by President Hoyte (of Guyana) that that was the one part of their training which they found to be beneficial to them on their return to their country. But all the other matters that we learnt particularly in our finals, because in Part I we had Contract and Tort and Roman Law – whatever that is –that in our final examination, we discovered that we could better have spent our time learning something about the constitutions of the Caribbean, learning something if we came from St. Lucia, or Dominica about the Napoleonic code and so on.

I will tell you my personal experience. There was considerable doubt, as we Westindians always underscore our own potential, as to whether we could produce people of quality here in the Caribbean by undertaking our own legal education. And there was in the early days, a certain amount of – I won't like to call it snobbishness, but lawyers are traditionally reactionary – and I used to say, priding myself on not being a reactionary lawyer which I probably was anyhow. The only thing was that I was less reactionary than the others that they ought to crown the lawyers with laurels and usher them out of the State. (I think that is what Cicero said he would like to do with the poets). Perhaps, I was a bit rash in my judgement, but later events proved that there was this reluctance on the part of some of our older practitioners to accept that all training here in the Caribbean could be as beneficial as that they had been exposed to in the United Kingdom.

When I returned in 1976 to a civil practice in Barbados, having become disenchanted with the criminal elements in our society, and having taken on at least three graduates from the Hugh Wooding and Norman Manley Law Schools – I discovered that they had a greater appreciation and a better concept of what the practice of law should be here in the Caribbean than I or any of my contemporaries had had.

Their training has been more relevant, it has one or two defects which I should not like to enter into here and now, but certainly, they have produced better attorneys – now I have avoided using the word 'advocates' because I think what we used to produce in the Caribbean with the English legal background was a variety of brilliant advocates, people who could dazzle a crowd of onlookers, or people sitting in a courtroom with their rhetoric.

I saw some of them graduate to becoming politicians. But when it came to a sound knowledge of office management, of what a lawyer's duty to the general society, the business community, and so on should be, I regret to say they were sadly lacking. I know one of my contemporaries who considered office business so irrelevant to the practice of law that his office was at the top of a staircase in a drugstore, and he had one chair. He could be seen with his gown flying, busying himself from court to court and he had a very successful practice, but he kept no books, so he never knew what he worked for, he never even knew if he had been paid for the cases in which he so brilliantly performed. I shall not call any names but I had to rescue that gentleman, organise his office for him so that he could be relieved for other duties. And one of those contemporaries of mine became a judge and he has the all time record of 15 years waiting for a judgement. I had the record I was waiting for the judgement and he was supposed to deliver it. And there was no prerogative writ that I could take out myself in order to enforce him to give a judgement, because in Barbados that would not be considered playing the game. I was very pleased, therefore, when two years ago, one of the graduates of the Hugh Wooding Law School brought a writ of *mandamus* against a statutory body – the Dental Association– in order to inspire them to enrol a qualified dentist on the register in Barbados – and that is the first time that I know in 40 years that anyone had had the courage to take out a writ of *mandamus* against a statutory authority in my country.

I referred just now to what I consider a defect. If you wish to involve practising barristers in the training of your students it will be necessary for you to set up here in Trinidad, in Port-of-Spain, close to the law courts, some kind of lecture facility whereby the practitioners will not have to spend two hours on the Eastern Main Road unless you give them special passes on the bus route, because no one is going to leave his office and spend two hours to come out to St. Augustine to find that the students have already gone home and, therefore, the students are being short-changed in this respect unless you have a lecture facility close to the offices of the lawyers. The

Norman Manley Law School in Jamaica is much better off in that respect and the members of the profession in Jamaica have pulled their full weight because they are not confronted with this ordeal of having to spend half the day on the road. This is something which I feel could be rectified.

The other defect which I should like to draw attention to is the question of attention being given to the abolition of appeals to the Judicial Committee of the Privy Council. I should like to confess that I am one of the back-woodsmen who fought strenuoulsy to retain the right of appeal to the Judicial Committee. And this was not based on any logic. But I had appeared before the Federal Appeal Court and it appeared to me that I bored the judges for two-and-a-half days and at the end of the first half-day, one of the celebrated judges asked me how long I had to talk and I told him that I had five points of appeal and I just finished the first point so by simple deduction I thought that I had two and a half days.

I was informed by His Lordship (whoever he was), we were then in October – that I could talk until Christmas – it was alright with them – that they had already written their decision. And this was a discipline in which neither one of the judges had been exposed to any kind of training at all because it was not a compulsory subject. So I spent my two-and-a-half-days and I had to go to the Judicial Committee, and I had the satisfaction of knowing that the five points that I had raised now constitute a leading case in the law reports in England reversing the Federal Court of Appeal. So I had, let me call it a gut sort of resentment, against having a Federal Court or a Court of Appeal in Caribbean being the final Court in which matters concerning my clients should be decided – and that was personal. But when I discussed the matter with the late Sir Hugh Wooding, he produced some statistics to me and he pointed out that, as of that time there had been thirty-three appeals to the Judicial Committee of the Privy Council and only two decisions had been reversed. One of them was the decision in the case in which I had been involved and I was right from the beginning. So let us say that there was only one out of thirty-two and you have to be impressed by that kind of statistics and Hugh Wooding said, 'Well if you are taking a one in thirty-two chance, there is no justification for making people spend the money to carry an appeal to the Judicial Committe.' And so I became converted by his logic.

The whole procedure of Appeals and getting leave to appeal to the Judicial Committee is a very tedious one and very expensive for the litigants unless you get permission to appeal in *forma pauperis*. So I think that we in the profession ought to give some attention, probably, to establishing our own Court of Appeal and having no limitation on the age of retirement of the judges because, in my humble opinion, when a judge attains the age of sixty-two or sixty-five as the case may be, provided he is physically fit, I think that he is at the stage where he has just begun to mature – he has just begun. We have had the cases of Oliver Wendell Holmes in the United States, the case of Mr Justice Douglas who became more radical as he got older (not to be confused with our own Sir William Douglas in Barbados). So you see there is a case for our having our own Court of Appeal. As a matter of fact, I should like to make it a qualification that no one under the age of sixty-five should be a member of that court, and therefore, in that way we would get the most experienced persons who will be available.

I made a promise when I started here this evening and I intend to keep it. The law schools themselves have to come to grips with these problems and change their programmes or amend their programmes effectively to meet the challenges of the profession in this day and age. Office management is going to involve more and more the use of computers, word processors, satellite and laser communications, micro-fiche in the search for not only records of property transfers, but also in the search of precendents of cases. When you go into a law library in the Caribbean and you look for a work which you wish to use in the arguments for your cases, you'll find that there has been one copy. Either the judge has taken it or the people on the other side have possession of it, and since we cannot all of us afford expensive law libraries, as a matter of fact, I do not know of any lawyer – no matter what pejorative statements are made about this – I do not know any lawyer who can afford the luxury of having a complete law library and at the same time own race horses – you have to have one or the other.

I should like to conclude in the words of Mr Wesley Williams who wrote in The Law – a Dynamic Profession – the American Bar Association Journal of 1955. Mr Williams is a member of the American Bar, the Pennsylvania Bar, and the Philadelphia Bar Association. He specialised in Corporation, Insurance, Commercial and Estate Succession Law. He said that the profession of the law must be a dynamic one. We cannot worship the status quo. It is the lawyer who has a competence to direct the progress of our remedial law. And if through apathy, indifference or fear of change he fails, we may be sure that others without the knowledge and experience and with little thought for the consequences will undertake this task.

174

Mr Chairman, My Lord Chief Justice, My Lords, Ladies and Gentlemen. I said right at the beginning that it was not my intention to do what I was being exposed to when I was admitted to the Bar by the Senior Bencher, Lord Henry of Moreton. There were only three of us from the Caribbean. My colleague from Trinidad, I understand, has two children who are also engaged in the practice of law. He is now, I understand two years deceased – but Lord Henry of Moreton admonished us that if we were going to be good lawyers that we should not get mixed up in radical politics and none of us took his advice. I should only like to advise you as graduates here today, that somehow or the other, there is a popular superstition that lawyers have a natural addiction, not necessarily qualification, for politics and if you are so inclined , if you think that in the pursuit of your careers that you can make some kind of contribution to your societies by taking up the challenge of the causes that lack assistance, against the wrongs that need resistance then I should respectfully like to submit that you will be fulfilling those high traditions which your predecessors in the Caribbean so successfully observed.

Thank you.

"The Caribbean is not an American problem"

Address to the 10th Annual Caribbean/Central
American Action-Sponsored (C/CAA) Miami
Conference on the Caribbean.
Miami, November 20, 1986

I wish to thank Mr David Rockefeller and the Caribbean Central
American Action for the invitation to attend the 10th Annual Miami
Conference and exposition on the Caribbean and to address the
luncheon today.

This is the first of these annual conferences that I have had the
opportunity to attend, because the past decade in which they have
been held, coincided with the ten years that the political party that I
am privileged to lead spent in opposition in Barbados. I emphasise
the word 'coincided' because I am sure that there was no connection
between my departure from office in 1976 and the institution of these
annual meetings.

One of the advantages of being in political opposition – and,
believe me, there are more than you may imagine – is that, free from
the daily demands of government, one has more time to look critically
at the working of our economic and political system. In the past few
years, I have given some thought to the evolving relationship
between the Caribbean and the United States of America and I must
confess that there are elements that have crept into that relationship
that frankly disturb me. I say this, without apology, as one who is
convinced that close co-operation between the Caribbean and our
neighbours in the Western hemisphere is both necessary and
desirable. The United States of America is not the least among these.
Indeed, our government has proclaimed the expansion of friendly
relations with the United States as one of the main goals of its foreign
policy. Yet, as I say, there are elements in the recent evolution of
U.S.-Caribbean relations that I find disturbing.

First and foremost, it seems to me that U.S.-Caribbean co-operation is being based – or at least being justified – increasingly on negative rather than positive considertions. Let me explain precisely what I am referring to.

If one examines many of the arguments used over the past few years, both by American and Caribbean persons, to persuade the American people of the desirability of assisting with the economic development of the Caribbean, one finds that essentially negative themes have tended to predominate.

If I may be allowed to summarise rather crudely, the case for cooperating with the Caribbean is put something like this: if the US does not help the Caribbean

(1) the communists, who are conveniently hiding behind every palm tree, will take over and surround the US with a ring of hostile islands;

(2) if the communists don't succeed, then the drug traffickers will take over and use the islands as bases to flood the US with 'dope';

(3) in either case, the entire population of the islands will flee to the US legally or illegally and take away jobs from American workers.

This may be a caricature but it is not, I suggest, a misrepresentation of the kind of negative reasoning that is frequently used to justify US-Caribbean co-operation.

The first thing that strikes one, or ought to strike one, about this line of reasoning is that it paints a terrifying, degrading and totally false picture of the Caribbean. For it suggests that what America has lurking offshore is nothing but a sea of troubles, with waves of disasters threatening your domestic tranquility. And unless one throws a whole lot of money and possibly guns at the situation, it might blow up in the face of the US. The cynical view, of course, is that in the context of American domestic politics such rhetoric is needed to 'sell' the idea of helping the Caribbean, to the American electorate. The problem is that you might end up believing such nonsense.

It is dehumanising and false to view the Caribbean as potential American problems. We are peoples with an identity and a culture and a history – the Parliament of Barbados will be 350 years old in 1989. We don't need lessons in democracy from anyone. However severe the economic difficulties facing the Caribbean, we are viable, functioning societies with the intellectual and institutional resources to understand and grapple with our problems. Collectively, we have the resource potential necessary for our continued development and, of course, we have a heritage of exquisite natural beauty entrusted to us. The Caribbean is, after all, a civilization.

The second thing that strikes one about the negative justification for American-Caribbean co-operation is that it paints a less than flattering portrait of the American people. Whatever the demands of political realism, it is, in my view, demeaning to suggest that Americans can be motivated to co-operate with their Caribbean neighbours only by fear for their own security. This is certainly not true of the many American tourists and businessmen I meet in the Caribbean. Indeed, the negative line of argument seriously short-sells the idealism, generosity, and sheer good sense of the American people.

In more practical terms, such negative considerations will tend to engender crisis-oriented and "quick-fix" attitudes to the region – attitudes which will be detrimental to the future of Caribbean-American co-operation.

There are many strong ties between the American and Caribbean peoples – ties of history, culture, and shared values. It is these positive considerations that should be emphasised as the basis of our mutually beneficial co-operation.

The second disturbing element that I have detected in the evolution of Caribbean-American relations is the trend towards an excessive reliance by the Caribbean on the US: the patronage mendicancy syndrome. The Caribbean is not the responsibility of the US, and it is totally unfair and unkind to Americans to ask them to shoulder all our burden. However poor we may be, however severe the economic difficulties we face, it must be clearly understood that the well-being and security of our peoples are our own responsibility. Let us face it, with all the money, all the technology and all the will in the world, the US cannot solve the problems of the Caribbean. In the first fifteen years that my political party managed the affairs of Barbados, we received no aid from the US of A, financial or military, neither did we ask for any. The US can contribute, and can contribute enormously, but only if the people of the Caribbean are themselves determined in a spirit of self-reliance to grapple with those problems.

The utmost priority has to be attached both by the Caribbean and the United States to the movement for regional co-operation in the Caribbean. For self-reliance in the situation of the Caribbean, must necessarily mean collective self-reliance.

Thus the most useful role that the US and other industrialised states can play in co-operation with the Caribbean is by strongly supporting multilateralism in the region and by channelling as much of their assistance as possible through the appropriate regional institutions. This approach offers the best prospects for self-sustaining development in the Caribbean.

It is a pity that the original multilateral approach to the Caribbean Basin Initiative (CBI) was never fully realised in practice, so that the CBI is now almost exclusively associated with the U.S. But I believe there is still hope for greater co-ordination of all the programmes of co-operation undertaken by various industrialised countries, such as Canada and the European Community with the Caribbean. Those same countries might also use their influence in the international financial institutions to get them to change their policies on lending to very small island states. Right now, because of an inflexible application of the per capita income criterion, access of the English-speaking Caribbean countries to soft loans from the International Development Association is being limited and several of them are being told that they will soon not be eligible for any type of loans from the World Bank. In the light of the serious economic difficulties facing the Caribbean today, this is a situation that is nothing short of shameful and demoralising.

I am convinced that the encouragement and support of multilateralism in the Caribbean, and among those friendly countries co-operating with the Caribbean, is the most productive and positive path to follow.

Let me say something about the CBI itself. I doubt that any similar initiative has generated such a torrent of words. Indeed, the CBI is a victim of its own rhetoric in that it has created expectations beyond anything that it could realistically be expected to fulfil. When one examines the actual Caribbean Basin Economic Recovery Act of 1983, one finds a very modest but useful effort at helping the Caribbean by providing restricted preferential access for Caribbean exports to the American market. And we really have to stop judging the CBI on what it ought to have or might have been. Political realism perhaps also dictates that with the Gramm-Rudman-Hollings balanced budget amendment, the current American trade deficit and the tide of protectionism sweeping the U.S., there is little prospect of getting Congress to improve the CBI. Thus, if the CBI is producing only very modest results, it is not because it is a failure, but because it is a very modest instrument. It is regrettable that the media in the Caribbean and the U.S. and our own medicant politicians find it convenient to forget that the whole concept of the Caribbean Basin as an object of economic development originated with the late Dr Eric Williams of

Trinidad and Tobago when he put forward his Caribbean Basin Plan involving one billion dollars to be raised totally from our own resources.

I can only say and say again to my friends in Congress: if you are serious about wanting to help the Caribbean, the best thing you can do is to allow all of our exports free and unrestricted access to the American market. Not as a matter of largesse or aid but as a means of redressing the unfavourable balance of trade which enures exclusively to the benefit of the U.S.A.

One area that offers considerable scope for growth in the Caribbean is the service sector. In a country as small and resource-poor as Barbados, the service sector is and will possibly become even more so a vital component of economic survival. Barbados has, therefore, developed both a tourism sector as well as an offshore sector designed to attract only legitimate business enterprises, whether bankers, foreign sales corporations or captive insurance companies.

Through our own tax treaty and tax information exchange with the U.S., we co-operate in the investigation of tax fraud and related illegal activities. The tax treaty was designed to strengthen economic co-operation between our two countries and any attempt to undermine the treaty will strike a severe blow at this co-operation. I, therefore trust that the U.S. government will honour its commitment to this international instrument and not take any action to alter the lengthily negotiated provisions of the treaty, for any action to alter the provision of the treaty would be a set back to investment tax co-operation and trade not only between Barbados and the U.S., but possibly between the U.S. and other Caribbean countries contemplating the signing of tax and information agreements with the U.S.

Upon assuming office in May of this year, my government commenced upon a programme of economic restructuring aimed at revitalising the economy of Barbados. Our economic policy goals were, and are, the reduction of high levels of unemployment, overcoming persistent economic stagnation; the restoration of private business confidence and performance; the curtailment of substantial losses in public sector commercial ventures and the rebuilding of export competitiveness.

The achievement of these goals has been tackled, initially, under the purview of budgetary measures which have sought to restore incentives to individuals to work, save and invest; reduce the costs of business operation; provide incentives to encourage reinvestment of capital; provide for business to build up healthy reserves, place resources behind small business and reduce the tax burden of private individuals and business.

Most salient of the measures was the reduction in the maximum rate of personal income tax from 60 per cent to 50 per cent; with all persons earning BDS$15,000 a year or less, being exempted from paying income tax. In addition the maximum rate of corporate tax was reduced from 45 per cent to 35 per cent, and will soon move to a graduated tax ranging from 15 per cent to 35 per cent. The tourist sector, in particular, was relieved of an onerous tax burden.

We took all these actions because we were convinced that the personal income and corporate tax regimes were stifling the creativity and entrepreneurial talents of our people, and also because of our firm belief that the private sector has a big role to play in bringing the economy back on track. The rate of return to the community of investment by the private sector is more efficiently realised, and that sector subsumes more importantly the individual working with his own hands.

These measures will, in the short run, generate substantial impact upon disposable income, demand for goods and services and the growth of government revenue from indirect taxation. Over the medium term the growth in purchasing power, correctly chanelled, will lead to the emergence of new businesses and expansion of those already established, thereby creating more job opportunities. Over the long run as businesses expand and new ventures develop, additional rounds of revenues and employment will be generated.

One other complementary area of reform which the government is pledged to undertake as a matter of urgency in order to restore economic health, is the problem of wasteful expenditure and inefficiency in the public sector generally and particularly in government-owned commercial enterprise. Our own enterprises policy recognises that government must play a role in the provision of private goods and services for purchase by individuals, and, therefore, government will continue to invest, appropriately in, and promote the production and distribution of private goods. However, we intend to put an end to the practice whereby publicly-owned enterprises, producing non-strategic goods and services are permitted to operate at a substantial loss with little likelihood of ever making a profit. In the extreme case where complete divestment is the appropriate course, such action will be taken.

Much of the infrastructural and institutional framework for business activity in Barbados was laid down during the years 1961 to 1976, when I had the privilege of heading the government of Barbados for three successive terms. Just as we in Barbados do not need instructions on the virtues of democracy, neither do we need instructions on the virtues of free enterprise. The government is committed to fostering the most healthy and positive climate for private sector investment, both domestic and foreign, in Barbados. We recognise that the ability to produce and export at internationally competitive prices will be critical to our success, and we welcome the foreign, and especially the American, investor, as one who can make an important contribution to that objective.

I look forward to close and friendly co-operation with the people of the United States during my tenure in office. I am convinced that such co-operation is to the mutual benefit of both the Caribbean and American peoples. But I feel equally strongly that such co-operation must be based on positive and not negative considerations and should reinforce the self-reliance and independence of the Caribbean. It has become fashionable in American domestic politics to invoke the name of Franklin D. Roosevelt in order to inspire Americans with a unity of purpose and vision and faith in this great country. I would urge that in the field of foreign relations, you also invoke the spirit of that great American statesman in dealing with your good neighbours in the Caribbean.

"Travelling down the road of social justice"

May Day Address to the Barbados Workers' Union
May Day Rally at Queen's Park, Bridgetown,
May 1, 1987.

Your Excellencies,
Mr President,
Mr General-Secretary,
Fellow workers, dear loving people,

This year, 1987, is of great significance to all workers' organisations in the Commonwealth Caribbean, since it marks the 50th Anniversary of the events that indisputably led to the legalisation and recognition of workers' organisations in the region.

A lot of young people here,and many more who may not be here today, may not be aware that prior to the year 1939, when the Trade Union Act and Trades Dispute Act were placed on the statute books, any organisation of workers, which set about to change their condition of labour were not only illegal at common law, but actions taken by workers, to bring about alleviation of their conditions, or to bring attention to their grievances, were liable to be crushed ruthlessly by the full impact of the penalties of the statute law contained in the Conspiracy and Protection of Property Act and other oppressive laws which reflected the social and economic prejudices of the times, and the fears which the political directorates of the day entertained in relation to the natural impulses of the masses to consolidate in order to seek redress to the many disadvantages which encompassed them at home and at work.

The Democratic League in Barbados with the Working Mens' Association, Captain Cipriani in Trinidad with his Working Mens' Association with which the Barbados organisation was affiliated, Hubert Crichlow in Guyana with his organisation, all surreptitiously, gave some leadership and opportunity to the masses to ventilate their grievances during the '20s and early '30s.

But when the voices of their leaders were stilled, and the economic pressures created by the Great Depression made life unbearable here in the Caribbean in the middle '30s, there was a spontaneous outburst of indignation on the part of the unrepresented and underprivileged of the region, which spread like a brush fire in the dry season, from the north in Puerto Rico to the south in Guyana, and from the east in St Kitts, to the west in Jamaica.

No middle class politician or professional person can either claim credit or responsibility for the events of 1937. The leaders who emerged after 1937, were not the supporters of Cipriani, Critchlow or O'Neal,* but rather persons whose consciences were jolted by the events in which so many innocent workers lost their lives at the hands of the militaristic cossacks, who held the thin red line of unenlightened British colonialism and imperialism.

Workers in Barbados were shot down for picking potatoes, by their own families in the police force. Similarly, in other areas in the Caribbean.

A commission under the chairmanship of Sir George Dean was set up by the governor of Barbados and in its report, the commission fully exposed the appalling economic conditions which prevailed in this country and which directly contributed to the uprising of the workers.

In other places, at other times, such assertions of the peoples of their fundamental rights have been glorified – sometimes quite justifiably –and enshrined in their histories as glorious revolutions. In France, in the United States, in Latin America, in the Soviet Union, in Mexico, and even in the Union of South Africa, this has been done.

Here in Barbados, our Barbadian teachers, appallingly ignorant of our own economic and social history, are continuing to teach our Barbadian children that we had riots in 1937. We committed unlawful acts by unlawful means so that the law enforcement agencies had to shoot hungry people digging potatoes, which they had not planted, in order that these law enforcement agencies might be able to maintain something called law and order.

If people in Barbados were not outraged, public opinion in the United Kingdom and elsewehere, was outraged. The British government appointed a Royal Commission under the chairmanship of Lord Moyne, who subsequently lost his life in the Middle East, to investigate the causes of the uprising; and that Royal Commission

*Charles Duncan O'Neal, founder of the Democratic League, and an uncle of Errol W. Barrow.

conducted its public hearings right here in Queens Park. The only days in my whole school career from the age of two-and-a-half in the American Virgin Islands, to age 19-and-a-half on the other side of Queens Park[**], that I have failed to attend in sickness or in health, or otherwise, was when I attended hearings of the Royal Commission here in Queens Park.

The commission did not publish its findings until after World War Two, as it would have been embarrassing to the British government if it had published its findings ... its report was submitted to the so-called 'Colonial Office' in which it recommended immediate legislation to establish trade unions in all the Westindian colonies; and that is how the Barbados Workers' Union was born.

The events of 1937, the protest of the leaderless workers, and not the submissions of middle class intellectuals or professionals, were directly responsible for the genesis of trade unions and trade unionism in the Commonwealth Caribbean.

I know because I was there. I was here, and I saw it for myself. I do not rely on the distortions of the workers' history with which this country has been afflicted in recent times, by persons who were not there, and were not interested at that time; and if they had been there, they would have run away, because they would not like to be associated with actions unacceptable to the social directorate of the era.

Mr President, Mr General-Secretary, compañeros, or compañeras, the union has come a long way in its 48 years – in its 48 unbroken years. There has been much social reform during this period. And just as important, the Barbados Workers' Union, has for a long time been internationally recognised.

In returning to the celebrations of May 1st, an order for which the Governor General signed in December 1986[***], the labour movement is showing its solidarity with the workers in 70 other countries who have adopted the designation of the first of May as a labour holiday which the Second Socialist International so designated as far back as 1889, 100 years ago.

In ancient times, May Day celebrated the return of Spring, with festivities and dancing. Today we are doing much the same thing. We are celebrating not the return of spring, but the return of hope which

[**]This is a reference to Harrison's College, a prestigious secondary school, located just outside Queens Park in Bridgetown, which Barrow and all Barbados' other political leaders have attended.

[***]In 1984, the previous Barbados Labour Party Administration shifted May Day celebrations to the first Monday in May, despite protests from the unions.

springs eternal in the human breast.

But I should like to say that the government of Barbados, which is a social democratic government, shares with the workers' organisations, the same objectives; and the main social objective which we share with the workers' organisations and why we find it easy to travel down the same road together, is the objective of social justice.

Social justice cannot be achieved in a society where there is inequality and discrimination either at the work place or outside of it. Social justice cannot co-exist with hunger and unemployment. No matter what achievement may be made by the workers' organisations in securing better conditions of work, better wages, better benefits for their members, as long as you have, outside of the workers' organisations, the industrial reserve army, as Karl Marx described it, or the unemployed, there can never be any social justice in the said society, even for those who are organised within the ranks of the workers' union.

I am submitting, and I think the workers' union has accepted, that it is the common duty of the government and the workers' organisation to see that the whole spectre of unemployment, as far as possible, is removed fom this society, in the first instance, and from the wider Caribbean association in the second analysis.

We are striving towards the elimination of want and distress. People who do not have jobs are a drain on those people who have jobs. Fortunately for us here in Barbados, we have still retained some of the survivals which we brought from our mother country. We have still retained the institution of the extended family. We have still retained those practices of looking after those less fortunate among us, even if they are remotely related to us, or not related at all.

So that I am satisfied that despite the fact that we have unemployment in excess of perhaps 18 per cent of the total labour force, that there are very few people, except your humble servant, who go to sleep hungry at night.

I go to sleep hungry at night by choice, and not be necessity. If I eat a heavy meal late at night, I cannot sleep; so mine is by choice. But I am happy to say that ... despite our indoctrination by the metropolitan cultures, we have managed to retain some of those ancestral practices in the society by which we ensure that members of the family are looked after. By the very token, we are impoverishing ourselves by having to feed those persons for whom the society is not creating the opportunities to feed themselves.

I am sure the Barbados Workers' Union, along with the other workers' organisations, are as much concerned over the alleviation of unemployment as we are as a government. It is very nice for one to get up on a platform and say that we want to relieve unemployment. But it is a far different thing to devise the instruments and create the social engineering by which unemployment is going to be alleviated, if not eradicated.

I do not have any ready formula. But what I want to say is that we are all concerned about it. In the past 12 months, unemployment has dropped by one per cent; but the labour force has increased by 4,000 persons. That really means that in the same period that over 5,000 jobs have been created. I do not think that the government would be so arrogant as to claim credit for having created all of those jobs. But by natural processes of economic growth, 4,000 more jobs have been created during the past 12 months which on the 28th of May would have been the 12 months that this government has been in office.

We are satisfied that we are making some progress in holding the line. But if we are going to reduce the 18 per cent to six or seven per cent, or an acceptable level in other words, then all of us have to work together to ensure that we do something in our own way to help those who are looking for jobs and who cannot secure them.

The government has taken steps by its budgetary measures to encourage the creation of jobs in the society ... The government has also established a task force, including representatives of the workers, in order to investigate ways and means by which we can create more employment opportunities in the society.

I am pleased to see here on the platform with me this afternoon no less a person than the Minister of Labour and Employment himself [Wes Hall]. Somebody criticised the government for setting up a task force to see if we can create jobs. They claimed that we said in our manifesto that we will create more jobs and when we called in all the branches of the society to help us, they say we did not know what we were doing, we had to ask other people.

I will deal with that particular approach to the problem of the society in which we live, because it is our desire to try to bring into consultation in all aspects of the management of this society, everyone who is engaged in the productive activity of the society itself, including the workers and including the employers.

No one group of persons in this society is endowed with all the assets, or the ingenuity whereby they have all the answers to all the problems in this society. We recognise as a government that in order to mobilise all the talents that we have in Barbados, we have to have consultation with all the people in the society all the time. We make no apologies for that.

Mr President, we are now in the last quarter of the 20th century... In the same way that by the social engineering brought about by devices such as National Insurance and Social Security, and by the insistent demands made by the workers' organisations that they should have a just share of the fruits of their labour, that the whole aspect of economic relationships in the society must undergo, and are undergoing a fundamental change.

I think that in the final 12 or 13 years of this century, the unions and the governments and the employers, have a very basic function to perform; that is, instead of regarding the elements in the society from the point of view of we the employers on one side, the government in the middle and the workers on the other side, we now have to look upon ourselves as all participants in the economic process.

The union now has to concentrate on training its members in management skills. That does not mean that I am advocating an immediate takeover of the commanding heights of the economy, as they used to be called in the 19th century, by the workers.

But I am looking forward to the gradual withdrawal of the government involvement in trying to bring about these changes and greater participation by the workers in the managerial functions of the society.

We are not going to achieve our common objectives of social justice if the workers are going to be there on the other side of the fence, having an antagonistic attitude towards the people who control the capital. We are only going to have harmonious relationships in this society if the people who now control the capital realise that the workers themselves are entitled to a share in the control of that capital, both in the managerial and ownership levels.

Therefore, greater shares in the businesses of the society must be available to the workers. Greater participation in management must be available to the workers and we have to abandon this concept that if a worker, through his exceptional talents manages to catch the eye of the selectors, the description that Wes***** will understand, and get a pick as a captain that he no longer can be regarded as a player and cannot take part in the union activities.

The captain must always be a worker himself. You cannot isolate a manager from the workers and say he cannot take part in the work, because my concept is that the manager is as much a worker as the

*****This is a reference to former Westindies cricketer and team manager, Wes Hall, who as Minister of Employment and Labour, shared the platform with Mr Barrow and union leaders during the rally.

man from whose ranks he sprung ... the employers must understand that if we are to have harmonious relationships in this society.

They are asking us now to subsidise the sugar industry. I do not want to go too far down that road, because 20 years ago, at a May Day meeting, I warned the workers in this country of what was going to happen and I was criticised.

I did not say what they said I said. But I warned the workers to watch out, that the thing was going downhill. But I am saying this: we want a share in the management.

They are now asking us the tax payers, you and me, to take up our money and subsidise an industry that is on its way out. But they do not want us to have a share in the management.

When we came into office in 1961 one of the first things that I insisted upon with the British government was that the workers' organisation should take part in the negotiations for the price of sugar under the sugar agreement, because they were getting up there behind closed doors as producers and negotiating with the British government for a price of sugar that would affect the level of wages that workers were to get here in Barbados, in Jamaica, in Guyana and Trinidad and Tobago. I put an end to that.

If year after year they are going to come to the government and people of Barbados and ask them to underwrite the losses of the Barbados sugar industry which we can ill-afford, then they must understand that we must have, for the workers, a share in the decision making at the very highest level, or no can do!

If your leaders are afraid to say it, I am not afraid to say it. I am not ashamed, as one of the former ministers told me, that I come from the plantocracy. I told him, yes, I come from the plantocracy. My grandfather did not take my grandmother behind any field of canes. He took her in church, and, therefore, I am not ashamed and, therefore, I can tell them that if they want the workers of Barbados to take part, to give up their hard earned taxes to support the sugar industry, all I am saying now 20 years later, is that we must have a share in the decision-making and look at the inefficiencies and the efficiencies of that particular industry.

What I say here today about the sugar industry applies to every single branch of economic organisation in Barbados and I say it without any compunction whatsoever. We have to change the whole aspect of economic relationship in this society, if we are going to move forward into the 21st century.

Otherwise, we are going to have this attitude: we are here in the pulpit and you are there in the pew, and you have to do what we tell you and listen to our interpretation of the holy scriptures.

So Mr President, Mr General-Secretary, brother workers, you did not come here to listen to a long speech from me. You came here to allow me to congratulate you on returning to the place where your organisation had its birth, here in Queens Park 50 years ago as a result of representations made by certain people. We should not forget the struggle of those early pioneers. We must not forget the representations made by Israel Lovell, and Roland Edwards; we must not forget the early sacrifices of people like Louis Sebro; we must not forget people like George Reid; we must not forget people like Claude Skeete, McDonald Blunt and others.*****

We have retuned to the cradle, and it is only by returning to our roots, that we will get the inspiration to go forward to greater and better things.

Thank you.

*****Editors note: Lovell, Edwards and Sebro were Workers' Rights Activists in pre-World War Two Barbados. Skeete was the third President of the Barbados Workers' Union and is credited with unionising the country's large corp of postal employees. Blunt was the union's second President, while Reid was one of its more recent activists.

Errol Walton Barrow (at right), returns to the Prime Minister's Office as leader of Barbados, just under ten years after his Democratic Labour Party lost office.

His new term as Prime Minister barely lasted a year, with his death on June 1, 1987.

Errol Walton Barrow (at left), strides into Parliament accompanied by Erskine Sandiford, who became Prime Minister with Mr Barrow's sudden death on June 1, 1987.

"Financial self-help"

Address to the Caribbean Development Bank Board of Governors' meeting in Grenada on May 13, 1987

Mr Chairman,
Fellow Governors,
President of the Bank,
Distinguished guests,
Ladies and Gentlemen,

This annual meeting is taking place at a time when there is a widespread interest in, and a dire need for the exploration of new initiatives and fresh approaches to the promotion of economic and social development in the Caribbean.

Last year, the Bank completed a comprehensive review of perform-ance and the outlines of a future role until 1990. Also of major significance was the statement of the President of the Bank[*] at the Sixteenth Annual Meeting in Caracas, Venezuela. That statement addressed the important issue of the place of people in, and their potential for contributing to, and benefitting from, the development process. These events coincided, more or less, with the return to office in Barbados of the political party which I have the honour to lead.

New fiscal and general economic management initiatives have been taken in Barbados which are designed to promote economic growth and long-term social and economic development. The government of Barbados has also been taking part in a series of new initiatives at the regional level, which are aimed at strengthening and advancing the integration movement, at a time when there is a renewed interest in the future of that movement.

The Caribbean Development Bank was established in 1970 as an instrument of regional development and regional integration, and to perform the roles of a development agency as well as that of a development bank. I first drew attention in 1963 to the need for such an institution in a speech made at the University of New Brunswick,

[*] Mr William Demas, a Trinidad and Tobago economist, and former Secretary General of the Caribbean community.

193

Fredericton, which was shortly afterwards read into the record of the Canadian Senate.

We, all of us here, have reason to be proud of the invaluable work done over the years by our institution headed and staffed by experts produced in the region. In recent years, the Bank has been striving to improve its performance in an unfavourable external environment. There is uncertainty over the prospects for higher rates of growth in the major industrial countries in the medium term. There is even greater uncertainty as to whether a return to higher growth rates in these countries will result in the spread of benefits and consequent stimulation of growth in the Third World, including the countries of this region. There is evidence to suggest that these major industrial-ised countries have been restructuring their economies in ways which will lead to internal growth and development. Resuscitation of these economies will not necessarily generate external spin-offs at a rate which used to be evident in past decades. Furthermore, the prospects for world trade do not suggest that the stimulation of international demand will necessarily bring benefits to small countries like ours, except if new exports are developed quickly which can be marketed on competitve terms. The prices of traditional Third World exports are unremunerative, while the prices of the goods they must buy are rising. The terms of trade continue to move relentlessly against the primary producers.

There is greater demand being exerted on our foreign exchange resources because of the need to service external debts. Foreign investment and capital inflows have been declining.

These problems have, in turn, brought trading difficulties at the regional level, as shortages of foreign exchange have led to increased protectionism.

I need not recount all the other difficulties facing the countries of the region. The staff and management of the Bank have done a commendable job in presenting these in the recent review of the performance of the economies of the borrowing member countries. What I should like to stress is that every indicator points to the need for urgent strategies which will move our countries and the region onto a path of self-reliant and self-sustaining growth if we are to prevent a further decline in the standards of living of the peoples of the Caribbean. We cannot sit passively and wait to reap the elusive beneifts of a return to growth by our major trading partners. Our efforts have to be redirected to internal restructuring and revitalisa-tion of our economies, in ways which will utilise more fully the indigenous human and physical resources of the region.

The Bank's document which outlines its future role through 1990 makes the observation that dependence on the traditional economic sectors will no longer work for the countries of this region. This observation can be extended further. Traditional strategies and measures will no longer work.

There is an emerging philosophy of development which could guide the Bank into a new and more effective development agency role and function. But the new strategy which is needed for our region will be valueless if people are not placed at the centre – both as a means and an end – of the development process. Such a strategy must rest on a confidence in the ability of the region's people to exploit our indigenous resources in a positive and socially profitable manner.

Greater importance needs to be placed on a basic needs and participatory approach to development in the region.I am happy to note that the leadership of the Bank is becoming increasingly aware of the importance of the full mobilisation and development of the human resources which reside in our wider communities, and of channelling these resources into the stimulation of economic growth and national development.

An approach which needs to broaden and enhance participation is in keeping with a policy of decreasing the role of government while stimulating the private sector – using the term 'private sector' in the widest sense.This is the policy which has been adopted by the government of Barbados. The strategy encourages the traditional private sector, but also seeks to elicit greater participation from smaller, community-based entrepreneurs and non-governmental organisations which are seeking to make their contribution in appropriate ways. Mr Demas called for such an approach when, in his statement at last year's annual meeting, he referred to '… the need for the entire society to give more attention to the expansion of self-employment and small-scale enterprises'.

The new strategy which we need must also seek to reform education and training programmes to impart new skills and upgrade old ones. Education and training programes should also be designed to promote a technological development which is appropriate to the industrialisation programmes of the countries of the region. Our educational systems are necessarily thirty years behind our require-ments because our educators are merely passing on what they absorbed thirty years ago. Who is going to educate the educators?

Sir, a strategy which focuses on enhancing the region's human resources and on harnessing those underutilised resources for greater contribution to the national development effort need not be costly. Excessive costs can be avoided, especially if collaboration is developed with those non-governmental organisations that are already involved with groups who are doing things in non-formal, appropriate and cost-effective ways. To this end, the bank should explore the possibility of developing supportive programmes with such non-governmental development organisations.

There is much self-help action which is taking place in our credit unions and co-operative movements, our workers' organisations, in farmers, women and youth groups who are participating in rural development programmes, programmes of literacy and adult education, running small income-generating projects and providing services like day care centres. With a little more help, the developmental contribution of these independent self-help initiatives can be maximised.

In short, Mr Chairman, the development agency function of the Bank needs to be turned in new directions, and a greater emphasis needs to be placed on this aspect of the Bank's activities.

Placing more emphasis on the development agency role and function of the Bank does not mean that the banking functions should be reduced. The Bank as a bank still has an important role to play in supporting such new strategies as can be devised to deal with the problems confronting the countries of this region.

Indeed, the banking role of the CDB assumes greater significance in the face of the pending graduation by the World Bank of some of the borrowing member countries. World Bank graduation will present the affected countries with challenges additional to those already created by the adverse international economic environment and the problems which are evident at the regional level.

On the bright side, however, World Bank graduation may yet point to another avenue which the CDB might explore to assist member countries to move along the path of self-reliance. There might be prospects for exploring with member countries ways in which increasing amounts of domestic and regional financing can be mobilised to lessen the demand for international lending. The way to respond to the decrease in World Bank lending is not necessarily to seek greater amounts of private and/or bilateral resources. Funds secured on such terms may only worsen the debt servicing problems faced by some of the member countries. The Bank needs to meet the challenge of pending World Bank graduation, by finding new and innovative ways in which the Bank's aid co-ordination services can be made available more readily to the member countries.

The challenge to help forge a self-reliant and self-sustaining strategy suggests that the Bank, as a Bank, also needs to look again at the ways in which available assistance is deployed. The need for new initiatives, such as the proposed Caribbean export financing mechanism is clear, as are programmes of lending through private and public sector financial intermediaries, for on lending to the private sector.

I should like to single out for particular mention and support, the call for increasing sectoral concentration of lending. Sectoral lending would allow for comprehensive consultative planning with respective governments and would help to identify project financing gaps which can be filled with effective aid co-ordination.

The role of the Bank as a bank will be threatened, however, unless an urgent solution is found to the problem of arrears. I observe that this problem remains grave and is more likely to affect the Bank's future financial viability. The arrears problem is a symptom of the economic dislocation from which some of the borrowing member countries are suffering. This problem needs to be tackled vigorously in the short term, but there is also the need for a longer-term perspective to be taken. The problem of arrears can only be dealt with effectively when the fundamental causes are addressed.

This is why the theme and focus of my statement have been the need for a strategy which promotes self-reliance and which helps to bring about internal economic restructuring.

In conclusion, Mr Chairman, I should like to record the appreciation of the Barbados government for the continued dedication to the service of the region by the President and staff of the Bank.

Thank you.

Prime Minister Errol Barrow (at rostrum), makes his final address to a Caribbean regional institution — the annual Board of Governors' meeting of the Caribbean Development Bank (CDB) in Grenada in May 1987. Mr Barrow died just a few weeks later, on June 1, 1987, of a heart attack at his modest west coast home in Barbados.

Other titles by Hansib Publishing

INDIA IN THE CARIBBEAN
Ed Dr David Dabydeen and
Dr Brinsley Samaroo
ISBN: 1 870518 00 4 PB   PRICE: £8.95
ISBN: 1 870518 05 5 HB   PRICE: £11.95

INDO-WESTINDIAN CRICKET
By Professor Frank Birbalsingh and
Clem Shiwcharan
ISBN: 1 870518 20 9 HB   PRICE: £7.95

THE SECOND SHIPWRECK:
INDO-CARIBBEAN LITERATURE
By Dr Jeremy Poynting
ISBN: 1 870518 15 2 PB   PRICE: £6.95

THE WEB OF TRADITION:
USES OF ALLUSION IN
V.S. NAIPAUL'S FICTION
By Dr John Thieme
ISBN: 1 870518 30 6 PB   PRICE: £6.95

BENEVOLENT NEUTRALITY:
INDIAN GOVERNMENT POLICY AND
LABOUR MIGRATION TO
BRITISH GUIANA 1854-1884
by Dr Basdeo Mangru
ISBN: 1 870518 10 1 HB   PRICE: £12.95

THE OPEN PRISON
By Angus Richmond
ISBN: 1 870518 25 X PB   PRICE: £4.95

COOLIE ODYSSEY
By Dr David Dabydeen
ISBN: 1 870518 01 2 PB   PRICE: £3.95

A READER'S GUIDE TO WESTINDIAN
AND BLACK BRITISH LITERATURE
By Dr David Dabydeen and
Dr Nana Wilson Tagoe
ISBN: 1 870518 35 7 PB   PRICE: £6.95

ESSAYS ON RACE, CULTURE
AND ENGLISH SOCIETY
By Dr Paul Rich
ISBN: 1 870518 40 3 PB   PRICE: £6.95

100 GREAT WESTINDIAN
TEST CRICKETERS
By Bridgette Lawrence and Reg Scarlett
ISBN: 1 870518 65 9 HB   PRICE: £10.95

BARRISTER FOR THE DEFENCE
By Rudy Narayan
ISBN: 09506664 2 4 PB   PRICE: £6.95

BOOK OF COMMONSENSE
Compiled by Neil Prendergast
PB   PRICE: £6.95

FROM WHERE I STAND
By Roy Sawh
ISBN: 0 9956664 9 1 PB   PRICE: £5.95

MY THOUGHTS, 2nd EDITION
By Pamela Ali
ISBN: 1 870518 06 3 PB   PRICE: £3.95

HOGARTH, WALPOLE AND
COMMERCIAL BRITAIN
By Dr David Dabydeen
ISBN: 1 870518 45 4 HB   PRICE: £15.95

THE GREAT MARCUS GARVEY
By Elizabeth Mackie
ISBN: 1 870518 50 0 PB   PRICE: £4.95

THE CARIBBEAN: GUYANA,
TRINIDAD & TOBAGO,
BARBADOS, JAMAICA
By Steve Garner
ISBN: 1 870518 55 1 PB   PRICE: £6.95

GREAT FIGURES FROM THE
THIRD WORLD
By Elizabeth Mackie and Steve Garner
ISBN: 1 870518 60 8 HB   PRICE: £11.95

THIRD WORLD IMPACT
7th EDITION
Edited by Arif Ali
ISBN: 0 9506664 8 3 PB   PRICE: £9.95
ISBN: 0 9506664 8 3 HB   PRICE: £13.95

RASTA AND RESISTANCE
FROM MARCUS GARVEY TO
WALTER RODNEY
By Dr Horace Campbell
ISBN: 0 95066 645 5 PB   PRICE: £6.95
ISBN: 0 95066 645 5 HB   PRICE: £9.95